To Bunny –

THE **B.E.S.T.T.*** LITTLE REAL ESTATE BOOK

EVER

*"I'll teach you how to fish,
so you can eat for a lifetime."*

You are the BESTT !

Ellen Boyle

ELLEN BOYLE

*Building. Exceptional. Salespeople. Through. Training.

Dedication

*To my dad, who taught me how to fish
so I could eat for a lifetime.*

*To my mother, who became my best friend
as we grew older and wiser together.*

*To my daughter, Dana, whose constant love
and support made this dream a reality.*

*To my sister, Anne, who has always been my
guide, mentor, and dear friend.*

Acknowledgments

Peggy Doepper, who has always believed in me and encouraged me in so many ways; Paul Breunich and Casey Jones for granting me the first opportunity to share the B.E.S.T.T. program with their company; Peter Helie for his strong leadership; Shirley Haner, Dian Vince, and Heather Lary for caring; Laurie Wright for hounding me to finish the book; Randy Friedman for her friendship and for introducing me to Anthony Parisi, my illustrator; and to Anthony, who captured my vision for the book cover; and to all of YOU who have allowed me to share, so that we can all be the BESTT.

It's not an accident or by chance that you are reading this book. It's all on purpose. In fact, just by reading this little book you will see that many things are going to change in your life. And it's all for the best.

I'll begin by asking you to think of yourself as a sponge as you read on. What I mean is for you to absorb what feels right for you. Use what you think will work in your life, and then squeeze out the rest for now. You may discover that what you didn't agree with at first will make sense at some later point.

Before we get into the secrets of success, I want to start by telling you a little something about me. This way you'll know that I don't just *talk the talk*, but I *walk the walk*. My story is sort of a rags to riches one. I remember all too well those days when I had to resort to using food stamps to feed my kids. It was both necessary and humiliating. I thank God those days are past. Today I "pay it forward" by donating 100 turkeys at Thanksgiving to poor families and supporting my favorite charities. I have been blessed with a thriving business in real estate that has awarded me financial freedom.

I grew up in a large middle class family in New England. I am one of eight kids. There was Mom, Dad, four girls, four boys, one bird, two rabbits and a dog. Although Mom always called us by our given name - and not a nickname - some of us referred to ourselves in order of our birth rank. #1 - my sister Anne - was the smart, pretty, and very popular one who loved reading and solitude. I was #2 and quite the opposite.

I loved being active and always on the go (often found playing sports with the neighborhood boys.) I always looked up to Anne. She has been a great teacher to me and encouraged me to discover my purpose.

The rest of the pecking order is as follows: Bill, Paul, Tom, Catherine, Marie and finally, Danny. I felt special having been blessed with many brothers and sisters. I learned so much from each of them and love them all dearly.

Mom and Dad were very smart. They had both graduated with honors from prestigious colleges. Mom was often referred to as a "walking encyclopedia." Dad was the "walking dictionary," and a master of words. They both believed in the power of knowledge and instilled in us the importance of education.

I didn't always see eye to eye with my parents, and I see now that those were the times when I learned the most from them. It reminds me of the quote from Mark Twain:

> *"When I was a boy of fourteen, my father was so ignorant that I could hardly stand to have the old man around. But when I got to be twenty-one, I was astonished at how much the old man had learned in seven years." – Mark Twain*

My dad was a very successful salesman and General Sales Manager for a large corporation. I was Daddy's little girl. Whatever Dad did, I did. I would be by his side, hammering and sawing with him when he built additions onto the house. I would listen to everything he said with great attention and full belief. After all, he was my Dad and he was my hero.

Whenever I wanted him to buy me something, Dad would answer, "I could buy it, but it would mean more if you earned it." He loved to recite the Confucius proverb…

> **"If you give a man a fish, he'll eat for a day.
> If you teach him how to fish, he'll eat for a lifetime."**

To earn money I did many odd jobs. For example, I was the first girl in town to deliver newspapers door to door. It was an everyday task, regardless of hot, wet, or snowy weather. I learned discipline and good work ethics. I also made pot holders and sold them to the neighbors for 25 cents apiece. I mowed lawns, washed cars, cleaned houses and did a variety of other things to earn money. I never minded the honest hard labor.

Then came the summer I wanted a new bike. This time I was really hoping Dad would simply buy it for me. All the popular kids were riding a sleek, 3-speed, black English bike. It was all the rage and I wanted one, too. I had a proposition for Dad that I thought would be a shoe-in to easily get the bike. I offered to wash and wax his car for the whole summer, if only he would P-L-E-A-S-E just *buy* me that bike. I vividly remember his positive reaction. His eyes widened and his face lit up. I was certain he would accept my offer. He patted me on the back and exclaimed, "This is your lucky day! I have a wonderful opportunity for you." He went on to tell me he had received a flyer in the mail from a Christmas card company looking for salespeople. It read, "SELL ONLY 80 BOXES OF CARDS AND *EARN* THIS 3-SPEED ENGLISH BICYCLE."

When he came home from work the next day he had the flyer with a picture of that beautiful bike. It was awesome! All I had to do was to **sell 80 boxes of Christmas cards**. (GULP.) The timing was great because the beginning of our summer vacation had just begun. Selling these 80 boxes of cards actually sounded pretty easy…

that was until after my first long day of knocking on doors. Then the reality set in. Do you have any idea how many people do not even THINK about Christmas in July? And, do you have any idea how many people don't celebrate Christmas?

Then there were the downright rude people who slammed the door in my face before I ever had a chance to show them the product. I hated the rejection. **But I had a goal.** I had taped the picture of that bike on the wall by my bed. Every night before I went to sleep I would stare at that picture. I would *visualize* myself riding the bike, and I was determined to make it happen.

By the end of that summer my persistence paid off. I finally sold the 80 boxes of those darned Christmas cards!

 I will never forget the day my beautiful, black, 3-speed English bike was delivered to the house. It was awesome! I knew then that the pain of selling was worth the gain. I rode the bike with a feeling of pride and accomplishment. I felt good about myself. I loved my bike and took excellent care of it every day.

It was a few weeks later when I overheard my younger brother Bill, a.k.a. number 3, asking Dad if he would buy him a bike like mine. Much to my surprise, Dad did just that! He simply bought Bill a bike without even making him work for it. I was blown away at first. Then I began to notice something. Over time, I observed that Bill never used his kickstand. He would throw his bike on the ground after a ride. He almost deliberately went through the puddles and over the rocks, and his bike was soon dented and dirty. (By the way, I did get permission from Bill to tell this story and he was okay with it. He is really a good brother.)

It was then that I learned two very valuable life lessons.

#1: I LEARNED THAT WHEN YOU WORK HARD FOR SOMETHING, YOU VALUE IT SO MUCH MORE THAN IF IT IS SIMPLY GIVEN TO YOU.

#2: I LEARNED THAT SELLING WAS THE HARDEST THING I EVER DID, AND I NEVER WANTED TO SELL AGAIN!

Fast forward several years . . . I grew up and married my high school sweetheart. After a long-term marriage, my once husband, now "wasband" turned me in for a newer model. I thought marriage was an institution that would last for a lifetime, but he didn't want to be institutionalized! He moved on, and I was left with four fabulous kids, no money in the bank, a lot of debt, and a broken heart. I had been primarily a stay-at-home Mom, or as I referred to myself, a "Domestic Engineer." I had a few part-time jobs, but really had focused most of my attention on caring for my family for over two decades. Suddenly, I had the responsibility of being the sole financial support for my family.

I'll never forget the afternoon when I sat in tears at the kitchen table, telling Dad about the divorce and the changes that were about to happen in my life. He always had the best advice for me, and I was now hoping for some pearls of wisdom for my new life. I told him I wanted nothing from my soon-to-be ex. I looked to him for the answer as to what I could do that would allow me to take care of the needs of my family while offering me flexibility.

Dad took my hand and looked me straight in the eyes then said, "Why don't you consider a career in real estate?" Blow me away! I looked at him like he had two heads. What on earth was he thinking? He knew I hated sales after the Christmas card thing.

He also knew I valued my reputation. I had lived in the same community for years and had developed a great rapport with everyone. My understanding of real estate agents was not favorable. In fact, I thought most real estate agents were hard sell salespeople with fangs, whose only purpose was to cement a deal at any cost. That sort of personality did not resonate with me, and I quickly dismissed the idea.

Seeing my reluctance, he leaned in closer to me, gently placed his hand on my shoulder, and with encouragement remarked,

"A career in real estate is an opportunity to help others with what is probably the single most important purchase or sale a person will ever make - a home."

He emphasized that I had the qualities and the abilities to be successful. He believed in me. I decided to follow his advice and signed up for the real estate course and became licensed in 1986.

Imagine - the very first company I interviewed with hired me on the spot. I was so excited and felt so special! At the time it was one of the largest and most successful companies in town. It wasn't long before I discovered that if you could simply fog a mirror, most real estate firms would hire you. Still in all, I was very excited about my new venture. I was eager to learn all that would help me to succeed in the business.

The market in 1986 was depressed, with many available homes for sale that weren't selling, a shortage of buyers, and interest rates in the double digits. My friends thought I was nuts to be getting into real estate, given the market conditions, and even doubted that I would make a go of it.

I knew I would succeed because I had a purpose. I wrote it on a small note card and tacked it on the wall by my desk. It read:

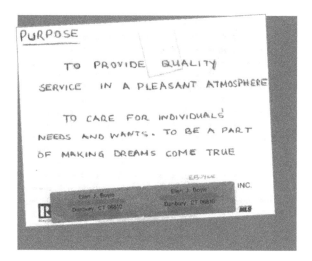

The owner of that real estate company noticed my Purpose Card and asked me what it was all about. I told him my reason for getting into real estate was to help others and to support my family. He was stern when he snapped at me and said, "You've got it all wrong! This business is totally about making money. That should be your first drive." I was really taken aback by his comment. I looked up from my desk and politely reminded him, "I am an independent contractor. This is MY purpose. This is the way I've chosen to conduct my business, and it is to help others. My reward for helping others will be financial."

I hated that company's misguided philosophies as well as the negative atmosphere. It was so uncomfortable in the office that I almost left the business altogether. It's very important to be happy where you work. Atmosphere will mold attitude, and a positive attitude is a major key to success.

Instead of leaving the business, I ended up leaving that company. I began interviewing with other firms and found a great fit with whom I remained affiliated for 20 years. As soon as I moved to the new company, my business exploded. I was in a regional office with over 45 agents. I ended my first year being recognized as the #1 Top Producer for homes sold and dollar volume for the office. I held that acclaim for the next two decades!

I had a great manager, Peggy, who was full of encouragement and inspiration and always had the right piece of advice for me. I recall a particular meeting with her to review goals and business planning. She had asked me to write a list of goals.

I wrote down only two words:

FINANCIAL FREEDOM

I was floored when I returned for my next goal review session with Peggy some 6 months later. She showed me a spreadsheet with my closed transactions and my year-to-date earned income. I knew my finances had improved because I had been able to pay all my bills in full, and on time. I even had some savings in the bank. I never really kept a record of what money I made because the focus was always on completing the transaction with a happy ending. I just kept on working. I was really shocked when Peggy handed me a transaction sheet showing my earnings for the year of over $80K. The next year my income doubled and so on. Life was great and it was the business that made it better!

I WILL SURVIVE

As life was stabilizing, the divorce was behind me, I had a steady income and I was happy, my next life challenge was about to surface. Out of the blue, in 1994 I was diagnosed with advanced breast cancer. My prognosis was lousy. I was sent home to get my affairs in order.

I underwent major surgery followed by 9 months of horrific chemotherapy. I really thought the "cure" was trying to kill me AND I wasn't about to surrender. After all, I still had kids in high school and I wanted to be there for graduations, college, marriages, and grandchildren. That's not to mention all of those families who were counting on me to sell their homes. I had a listing inventory of 57 homes that I was managing, by myself. I didn't have an assistant to depend on or a backup to do the work for me. As one listing would deposit, another new listing would come along. All these people were counting on me to sell their homes. I had no time for the illness. I had no time to die! More importantly, I had many reasons to live.

There were many variables that helped me through those dark days including my family, friends, my faith and my business. I could focus thoughts on helping others and didn't have time to feel sorry for myself. Being blessed with a huge real estate business gave me a much-needed distraction from reality.

Call me crazy, but I actually put a deal together while in the recovery room. I felt great because this was a foreclosure I had been watching for a long time. The buyers were first-time homebuyers and the home was just what they wanted. We could have lost it if we waited another day.

Truly, I had my challenges that year, but I also had some great achievements. 1994 was the first year of many that I was recognized as the #1 Selling Agent in the entire company (over 500 agents.) Throughout that year I felt it was ME vs. THE BIG 'C' (Cancer). It was then I realized that I was winning the battle!

I set my next goal to be #1 in the company for closed units. I would need to close over 80 homes to do so. I actually surpassed that goal and closed 108 for the year. Remember, I didn't have an assistant and I didn't work in a team. It was just me. Because I had a clear, written goal I was able to achieve it. I began closing over 100 transactions annually and enjoyed a vacation every six weeks. You'll learn my life management techniques later in the book that can help you do the same and more.

I was asked by my company to share some of my techniques with the new agents as a segment of their training program. That developed into my being hired as their Director of Training. I loved sharing with others in hopes of helping them build their business. Their success became my success. I made the transition from helping my clients, to helping thousands of agents help their clients buy and sell homes. I got such a rush watching all these people build their business using my "secrets."

The real secret is that these are not secrets, but integral business practices that every top producer is using. You see, for many years I had been gleaning information from top producers throughout the country. Every time I read an article in a real estate magazine that was written by a salesperson that I found interesting, I would contact that person and pick their brain. I did this to build *my* business, never realizing at the time that I would later be passing this information along to so many others to help them build their business.

I often questioned things that happened in my life and wondered if there would ever be an explanation that would make sense. I finally had my epiphany, or as Oprah Winfrey would call it an "Aha" moment. That's when you take a good look at your life and discover your purpose. Suddenly, I understood why I had to experience so many lessons and why I had to go through so many hard times. I used to wonder why I was able to develop a successful career in real estate while others struggled.

Suddenly it was all clear.

My purpose IS to:

ENLIGHTEN, EDUCATE AND ELEVATE OTHERS TO THEIR HIGHEST POTENTIAL.

I knew I wanted to teach others. I wanted to change course and develop a new career. I would step out of my comfort zone and share with others what I learned over the years. I would get enjoyment watching others prosper by simply using the tools of knowledge I would supply.

About this same time, my older daughter, Christine, was looking for a way to stay at home with her girls and still be able to afford the mortgage. I encouraged her to become licensed in real estate and offered her a partnership with me. She decided to follow in my footsteps and became a successful real estate agent in her own right.

Also, around the same time my younger daughter, Dana, moved back to our hometown for a while and offered to help with my classes. She is now my VP of Operations for all my classes and she is my rock. All the pieces had fallen into place.

So there you have it. I am just an ordinary person who, with the right tools, has become extraordinary in real estate. I say this to you with humility in my heart. I hope that you will use what you read here to change your life and your business.

THE STORY OF THE NUMBER 8

I want to take a moment to tell you a bit about the number 8. I do not study numerology, however, I do pay attention to things that come into my awareness. When I learned about the number 8 and its meaning,

I knew I wanted to use it in my work. My classes and teachings often revolve around the number 8, and here is why.

According to the studies of numerology, the number 8 represents *power, business, success, position, reputation, and* **money**. The number 8 takes its energy and expends it forcefully out into the world. Number 8 wants recognition, authority, tangible achievements, and clear evidence of respect and self-mastery.

All of these meanings could relate to us, both in our lives and in our business. Don't you agree?

I liked this idea of the number 8 and, therefore, there are 8 doors (chapters) in this book. All I ask is that you enter each door with an open mind. You will discover the power of knowledge.

It will work when you work it. So let's get working!

Believe in Yourself

"No one can make you feel inferior without
your consent." - Eleanor Roosevelt

It all starts with YOU.

YOU – YOU – YOU – <u>YOU</u>

It is time for a little exercise. Work with me on this. Put down the book just for a minute and get a mirror. Now look into the mirror. I mean... REALLY look into the mirror.

Who do you see? You are beautiful. Look deep into your eyes, as they are the windows to the soul. See only the perfection. You may be thinking that this is crazy, but do it anyway.

> *In order to perform as a dynamic salesperson you must first believe in yourself.*

Begin each day with DAILY AFFIRMATIONS.

An affirmation begins as a positive statement in your mind. When repeated daily it moves into your heart as a knowing that manifests into reality.

Repeat these words aloud and use them as DAILY AFFIRMATIONS.

- I am a good person.

- I care about others.

- I love what I do.

- I am the best at what I do.

• My reward for helping others is financial freedom.

• I am happy.

• I am healthy.

• I am loved.

• Create your own affirmations and go on.

 A great example of affirmations is the story of *The Little Engine That Could*. It is a kid's story that I feel applies to adults. It's about a little engine that was overloaded with the circus and needed to get up over a huge mountain. Waiting on the other side of the mountain in excitement for the circus were lots of little boys and girls. The load was heavy and the little engine didn't want to disappoint them. The engine started the upward journey by saying, *"I think I can. I think I can. I think I can."* It huffed and puffed and chugged and chugged as it became more difficult to climb the mountain and then it began to say, *"I know I can. I know I can. I know I can."* And then, with the encouragement of all the clowns and animals in the circus it said, *"I can. I can. I can."* It got to the top of the mountain and easily rolled into the town and made all the little boys and girls happy.

The story of *The Little Engine That Could* reminds me of the real estate business. All too often we are overloaded with challenges. Many people start their career by saying, "I think I can, I think I can, I think I can." Those who continue to affirm, "I can, I can, I can," will succeed.

Losers never use affirmations and will give up before getting anywhere. This is a tough business and there may be negative diversions along the way. There will be people that will have you questioning if this is the business for you. You must keep the courage of your convictions and keep on chugging along saying,

"I KNOW I CAN. I KNOW I CAN. I KNOW I CAN."

It's imperative that you take some silent time to go deep within yourself. Understand the importance of what we do for a living and how we can make a tremendous difference in the lives of others.

> *You must go within or you will go without.*

Someone who shared wonderful teachings of self-empowerment was Dr. Wayne Dyer. Sadly, he passed in 2015. I was an admirer and student of Dr. Dyer for years. I attended many of his lectures and even met him in person. He was a very gifted human being. I would suggest for you to read any or all of his books and learn how to discover your inner self. This is not "New Age" thinking, rather it is what I would call "Today" thinking.

What is "New Age" anyhow?

A quote from Ralph Waldo Emerson reads:

"The first thing we have to say respecting what are called new views here in New England, at the present time, is that they are not new, but the very oldest of thoughts cast into the mould of these new times."

This was from a lecture read at the Masonic Temple in Boston in 1842. So you see, this is simply an old thought being cast into today's time.

Once you have the strong belief in yourself and are using your daily affirmations to reinforce those beliefs, it's time for the next step. . .

DISCOVER YOUR PURPOSE

If your purpose in real estate begins with helping others, then you are right on track. I believe that a career in real estate is a vocation, and not just a job. It's almost like a "calling."

This business becomes a part of you and you become a part of it. A regular job is 9 to 5 and you can leave it at the office. In this business you get into people's lives and help them. Remember how I told you early on what my Dad said about real estate?

"Real estate is about helping people with what is probably their most important purchase or sale they will ever make – a home."

I came across this writing from an unknown author that pretty much sums up what we do:

TODAY. . .

Someone needs my help to sell a home... not just a house. Chances are they've lived there, loved there, and despite the faults of the house or the owners, it's a home.

To them, I PLEDGE the respect that I would want others to have for my home and for the members of my family.

Someone needs my help today to find a home, not just a house. A new home can mean new hope for... a new opportunity, a new job, a new marriage, or a new start. A new home can bring the peace, happiness, joy, friends, and love they picture for themselves in the shelter of their home.

I'm going to help someone TODAY.

Not many people get the opportunity to help others in times so dear to life. Yet, I DO, and I CAN, and I WILL, for their sake and for MINE!
                                        - Author Anonymous

We have a huge responsibility in helping people to change their lives, whether it is a home purchase, sale, or rental. When you fulfill your purpose of helping others, you will receive a reward for doing so. Besides the personal and business gratification, you will also earn an income, which is important.

There is nothing wrong with making money. In fact, there is nothing wrong with making a lot of $$$$$$. It's what you do with the money that matters. I suggest reading the book *The Diamond Cutter* by Geshe Michael Roach. It's a bestseller with strategies for managing your business and your life, and is read by highly successful business people. Geshe Roach talks about three guiding principles he used in New York City to build a diamond business from nothing into a worldwide operation generating many millions of dollars a year. To quote from his book, those three principles of a successful business are as follows:

"The first principle is that the **business should be successful: that it should make money**. There is a belief prevalent in America and other western countries that being successful and making money is somehow wrong for people who are trying to lead a spiritual life... In fact, a person with greater resources can do much more good in the world than one without. The question, rather, is how we make the money; whether we understand where it comes from and how to make it continue to come; and whether we keep a healthy attitude about the money.

The whole point, then, is to make money in a clean and honest way, to understand clearly where it comes from so it doesn't stop, and to maintain a healthy view toward it while we have it.

The second principle is that **we should enjoy the money....**

The third principle is that you should be able to look back on your business, at the end, and honestly say that your years of doing business have had some meaning...and the most important part of the business – at the end, when we are looking back on all we have achieved – we should see that we have conducted ourselves and **our business in a way that had some lasting meaning, that left some good mark in our world."**

I came into this business to help others and am rewarded handsomely for doing so. I have left a good mark on every life that I have touched and continue to build lifelong relationships. Do you feel the same?

Hopefully, by this point you are moving inward to a wholesome place of Self-Belief...

Time for a pop quiz ...

Question:

WHO DO <u>YOU</u> BELIEVE IS THE <u>BEST</u> PERSON TO SERVE THE PUBLIC WITH THEIR REAL ESTATE NEEDS?

What's your answer?

Say it out loud.

I can't hear you…..

If you just said "I AM", then you are right.

Now repeat, "**I AM THE BEST, I AM THE BEST, I AM THE BEST…**" over and over again until you believe it to be true.

This way of thinking has nothing to do with ego or conceit. It is all about being YOU.

You must have a strong belief system in place to enable the SECRETS OF SUCCESS to work for you.

WHEN YOU BELIEVE IT, YOU WILL SEE IT!

WORKING EXERCISE

Sit up straight. Take 3 deep breaths, in through your nose and out through your mouth. Look straight into a mirror repeating these words:

I AM SUCCESSFUL.

I LOVE EARNING MONEY.

I AM THE BEST AT WHAT I DO.

I AM HONESTLY HELPING OTHERS.

LOTS OF MONEY IS COMING TO ME.

I AM ABUNDANT.

I LOVE WHAT I DO.

It's a wonderful feeling to love what you do.
Remember this, when you love what you do,
you'll never work another day of your life.

Goal Setting

"There are no shortcuts to any place
worth going." - Beverly Sills

Establish Personal and Business Goals

Goal setting is what separates the ordinary from the EXTRAORDINARY. When you have a goal, you have a reason to be. Goal setting is a powerful process of thinking about your ideal future and motivating yourself to turn the VISION into REALITY.

Goals are not get-rich-quick schemes. Goals are not instant success stories. A goal cannot be met without taking concrete steps. You see, some people want to succeed and others are determined to succeed. Goals make it happen.

Don't confuse goals with dreams either. Although dreams often set the stage for goals, they are only thoughts that must be followed up with goal setting.

Where have you been and where do you want to go?

In your ideal world, what would you be doing right now?

What do YOU want to achieve?

What would make you happy now and always?

Make a goal plan. This plan will be the road map to your desires. If you took a road trip from Maine to California, you would need a map or GPS to get you there. Without direction, you could be driving aimlessly and take much longer to get to your destination. Think of your GOAL as a road map to your life.

This simple method for goal setting works well and all you need to do is to follow it. Your goals must be **written, specific,** and **realistic.**

SMART is the acronym often used to help us remember how to set our goals.

- **S**PECIFIC
- **M**EASURABLE
- **A**TTAINABLE
- **R**EALISTIC
- **T**IME FRAME

Step one, **write** your goals on paper in large print. Achievement of your goals happens more often when they are written. In a study of Harvard graduates, the 3% who had written goals achieved more financially than the other 93% combined.

Step two, make your goal **specific**. By specific I mean detailed. For example, if your goal is to buy a new car then specify the make, model, color, year, even including the accessories. Then set a date for the purchase of that car.

Step three, **speak** your goals aloud daily. When you wake up in the morning, take a few minutes to say out loud what you want. Speak to the mirror so you are speaking this to yourself.

Remember, your goals MUST be achievable. This is the most important part of the process. Try to avoid making a goal for something that may be unrealistic. This could be self-defeating and deflate you before you begin. You CAN reach for the stars, if you can see a way to get to them.

It is proven that those who follow this principle of goal setting will accomplish their goals!

I'd like you to make a new personal goal right now. Get a photo or a poster of something you want or of a special place you would like to be. Have that photo displayed where you can see it every day. Tell yourself it is possible for your dreams to come true. Stop using the word *impossible*. Try modifying your vocabulary starting with the word impossible. Change the impossible into POSSIBLE.

IMPOSSIBLE → I-AM-POSSIBLE

Scientists used to say that it was impossible for metal to float. Today, the United States of America boasts the largest fleet of ships in the world, all made of metal!

Achieving your goals requires determination. You may experience some setbacks. That's okay. Just pick yourself up and continue to move on. Don't ever be afraid of failure. Some of the most successful people in history failed before they succeeded.

- Babe Ruth struck out 1,330 times, but he also hit 714 home runs.

- Walt Disney was fired by a newspaper editor for lack of ideas. He also went bankrupt several times before he built Disneyland.

- Albert Einstein did not speak until he was four years old and didn't read until he was seven. His teacher described him as "mentally slow, unsociable, and adrift forever in his foolish dreams." He was expelled and was refused admittance to the Zurich Polytechnic School.

How often have you heard, "A journey of 1,000 miles starts with the first step?"

Set small goals first that will lead to the big ones. If you want to lose weight, don't say you want to lose 50 pounds in two weeks. Rather, tell yourself you will lose 2 pounds this week. Then add another 2 pounds, and so on. This helps you to stay on track and again, is *achievable.*

Enjoy your accomplishments. This all builds self-confidence which is an added bonus for achieving your goals.

Know that your goals will change with time and life. Adjust your goals regularly to reflect your experiences and knowledge.

KEY POINTS

Goal setting is an important method of:

• Discovering your purpose

• Working to achieve your purpose

• Building self-confidence

• Validating the meaning of your life

• Making your dreams come true

Life Time Management

"Society is always taken by surprise by any
new example of common sense."

\- Ralph Waldo Emerson

People are often curious about my life/time management tips and tools. They wonder how it is possible for me to close 100 transactions annually, take a vacation every six weeks and enjoy my life. They would ask about my time management skills. First, none of us can manage time. Time is always in motion and has its own mission. We can, however, manage our life. I refer to this process as LIFE MANAGEMENT. Here are my secrets of success for life management. They are very simple and basic, yet many do not follow them. Try to work life management and enjoy your life.

- Have a MASTER PLAN. Plan each day hour by hour.

- Block out one hour daily for mailings and farming.

- Block out time for returning phone calls.

- Use a Day-Timer, smartphone, or paper organizer. Try not to have little notes everywhere that can get lost or misplaced.

- Use a To-Do List.

- End each day by reviewing your To-Do List and check off what you have accomplished. What you didn't get to today needs to be at the top of your next day's list.

- Work during your periods of high productivity. Some people work best in the morning, some in the afternoon. Find your high energy time and work then.

- Act on a thought as soon as it comes to your mind - "I need to call a client to give them a status report." DO IT NOW while it's fresh in your mind.

- Keep a notepad handy for those thoughts that you can't get to immediately.

- Get quick projects done and out of the way first.

- Do first what you really want to do last. If you leave a difficult call until the end of the day, it will shadow your whole day.

- Allow more time to complete a project than you think you need.

- BE ON TIME! If you are often late, try setting your clocks or watch ahead.

- Organize using the F.A.T. process - File It, Address It, Toss It!

- Under-promise and over-deliver.

- Use a highlighter to notice important data.

- Use a device to record and make note of important thoughts.

- Use your voicemail to the fullest extent to stay focused. Don't lose your train of thought. Let people leave a message and call them back so you can hear their tone and have information ready ahead of time.

- Become educated on the latest computer technology as needed for online information and research.

- Take each project to completion before beginning another.

- Put a "**Do Not Disturb**" sign on your desk. This lets people know that you are busy and can't talk right now.

- Delegate responsibilities - hire an assistant.

- Form a team with a few other associates.

- Steer clear of negative people, they will only pull you down.

- "Know when to hold 'em and know when to fold 'em. Know when to walk away, know when to run." Yes, Kenny Rogers was right when he said this! Get rid of 'dead wood.'

- Keep important files with you.

- Keep work supplies in your car.

- Pretend each day is like the day before vacation.

- Make an appointment with yourself each day. Take time for you!

Again, this may sound basic, but basics are what it takes. Get back to the basics to streamline your business!

Sales and Branding

"As a sales professional you must realize first and foremost that you do not sell products and services. You sell what those products and services will do for the people you serve." - Tom Hopkins

New Age Selling in a
"Shifting Market"

It's been said that sales is the oldest profession in the world. Many of the basic sales traits have been forgotten. We must get back to the basics! We don't need to reinvent the wheel, but the highly successful real estate professionals know how to spin "that ole wheel" to stay on top of the market.

There are two types of sales approaches. There is the "hard sell" and then the "soft sell." I am sure you are familiar with the "hard sell" approach and probably don't like it any more than I do! It's full of pressure and all about a quick closing with no concern of repeat business. It's all about SELL, SELL, SELL.

The second type of selling is called the "soft sell" approach. This is what works in real estate. The soft sell approach has to do with counseling instead of just selling.

Although I have closed over 100 transactions annually, I've NEVER really SOLD a home. What I mean is I sell the town, the location and features of the home. People BUY the homes and no one wants to be pushed into buying that home. Rather, it's our job to help them make good business decisions. We can accomplish this through the use of tie-downs.

Ask questions beginning with the word **WHAT, WHERE, WHY, WHEN, HOW, IF, IS**. Examples of powerful tie-downs are:

• **What** is it about this home that you like?

• **Where** would you like to see yourself living?

• **Is** this what you are looking for in a home?

• **How** would you feel if you lost this home?

• This **is** what you're looking for, **isn't it?**

• **Does** this home offer **what you want?**

• **If** you could get this home for the right price **would you want to make an offer now?**

• **Is** there something about this home that you don't like?

• **Would** you be happy here?

By utilizing these tie-downs you can help your buyers make great business decisions and they'll feel like they are making the decisions on their own.

Remember the Golden Rule with these tie-downs: **Do unto others as you want them to do unto you.** Spend extra time listening to what people have to say. It's been said that salespeople were given two ears and one mouth so we would listen more and speak less.

According to NAR statistics, one of the biggest complaints people have with their real estate agent is that they don't listen. It is so important to BECOME A GOOD LISTENER. When you pay attention to what someone else wants, you will be working smarter, not harder, to help them make their dreams come true.

I once had an agent comment on how he showed 50 homes to one buyer. My first thought was that this agent was lacking in sales skills. He probably did not listen to the client and he probably had no closing skills. I'll get into this in-depth in an upcoming chapter on working with the buyer. The bottom line is there was a communication problem here.

There are times when agents have told me they do not work with renters. I couldn't understand why they felt that way. I believe that anyone who needs my help to find a home, whether renting or buying, is important. Furthermore, renters often become buyers and form the foundation of your business base.

I have a great story to relate on how renters turn into buyers. Early in my career I was in the office catching up on paperwork when three young men walked in looking for a one-year rental on the nearby recreational lake.

The duty agent pulled me aside asking if I wanted to take these customers. I had a reputation for accepting any business thrown my way. She said she didn't work with renters. I got the feeling she thought it was beneath her. She added that working with these guys would be a waste of her time. Then she warned me that it would be almost impossible to find a landlord who would rent to three single men. I took the challenge!

As it turned out, all of these men had excellent corporate jobs. I found them the perfect rental house located on direct waterfront. They were very grateful to me for taking the time to help them find a place to live when other agents wouldn't give them the time of day.

They loved the house and they loved me. They turned out to be wonderful tenants. I earned $600 for my efforts and felt great about helping the clients find a home. The landlord was so pleased and promised never to forget me.

I stayed in touch with these men and periodically checked in with the landlord.

The story doesn't end there... One year later, all three men had become engaged to be married. Their lease was ending and they needed homes. Since I had kept in touch, and they had a positive experience with me, they all purchased their homes with my help.

Better yet, their landlord was tired of renting and hired me to sell his lake house. The house was an expensive property that sold for a high price.

From one rental I got FOUR pieces of return business. I also developed relationships with people who liked the way I worked and would refer me to their friends. You can see how one rental can mushroom into millions of dollars of earned income and a business base.

Be careful not to judge people. Be careful not to discriminate. Treat everyone equally and you'll never have to worry about breaking the Fair Housing Laws.

SELLING YOURSELF –
CREATE YOUR UNIQUE BRAND

Branding and sales go hand in hand because in order to effectively conduct your business, your perception of who you are is very important. This perception is created through branding.

The American Marketing Association (AMA) defines a brand as a "name, term, sign, symbol or design, or a combination of them intended to identify the goods and services of one seller or group of sellers and to differentiate them from those of other sellers."

Therefore, it makes sense to understand that branding is not about getting your target market to choose you over the competition, but it is about getting your prospects to see you as the only one that provides a solution to their problem.

The objectives of a good brand are to:

- Deliver the message clearly.
- Confirm your credibility.
- Emotionally connect to prospects.
- Motivate the buyer.
- Cement user loyalty.

Branding and marketing **YOU** is often neglected, when it should be highlighted. In order for the public to know you are in business, they have to see you constantly. You must become an expert at branding **YOU**. This is one of the best ways to ensure repeat business.

Branding costs money. Agents are reluctant to spend money. Please know that "money makes money." It is suggested to allocate about 10% of your income to personal marketing and promotion.

Don't expect your company to market YOU. They are spending their monies marketing THEIR BRAND. To rephrase what President John Kennedy once said…"Ask not what your company can do for you, ask what you can do for your company." You're an independent contractor so your company is **YOU**.

Ideas for Branding YOU...

1. Put a photo of you in every ad, whether print or online. Be sure it's a recent picture and not one that was taken when you graduated from high school (unless you just graduated from high school.) Update your picture yearly. Do NOT use a glamour shot. You are beautiful just as you are!

2. Have a personal website with all your contact information. Update the site regularly. Many companies offer a personal page on their website. Be sure to keep this up-to-date and offer information about yourself as well as a photo.

3. There are many free online websites such as Facebook, LinkedIn, etc., that offer ways for people to find you, including additional information about you. Utilize as many sites as possible for great FREE networking.

4. Advertise in real estate magazines because they offer shelf life. (I don't recommend TV or radio ads. They're very expensive and not as effective as print ads. Most importantly, they do not have a shelf life.)

5. Advertise in the newspaper, either in a display ad or in the classified section.

6. Advertising must be done consistently for it to work. Set a schedule and budget for ongoing advertising. You can even try splitting an ad with fellow agents to reduce the total cost.

7. Try to find reciprocal advertising options, like sharing website links with mortgage or home inspection companies.

8. Other effective self-marketing resources are novelty items such as, personalized refrigerator magnets, calendar magnets, pens, notepads and many others. These marketing items have shelf life. I love Magnets USA and direct you to their website for products at www. magnetsusa.com. They offer a large selection at great value.

I've got a great success story about business card magnets and how effective they are in making you money. I was only in the business for a few months when Dad told me I needed to buy business card refrigerator magnets to promote myself. The magnets were going to cost $225 which sounded like $2 million to me at the time. Dad told me it was really important to invest in my business. You know by now that I often took Dad's advice, so... I ordered the magnets.

I handed out magnets at every opportunity possible. Every Open House, every person I met, and in every envelope I mailed, my magnet was there.

I got a call one day from a man whose name I did not know, although I did recognize his address. I knew the address because several years ago I had been the listing agent for that property. However, I was NOT the selling agent. His conversation was brief and he simply said, "I'm calling for you to list my house and you are the only agent I will be calling." Yeah, that was a great call!

When we met, I asked him what made him call me and not his selling agent who was still in business. He said he called his agent shortly after closing on the property. He left several messages requesting a copy of the plot plan and never got a response.

After getting frustrated, he called my office leaving the same message asking for a map. I sent him a map of the land and included in the envelope one of my magnets. He showed me the magnet that had been stuck on his refrigerator for three years. He said he thought of me every day when he saw my picture and felt as though we were friends.

I listed the house and it sold for $460,000. He and his wife used me four more times over the years to list and sell their homes. That one magnet earned me thousands in commissions!

This is only one of dozens of magnet stories that have all paid off. Once again it proved...Father Knows Best.

DO NOT BE A SECRET AGENT

The best way to sell yourself and make money in this business is to let everyone you come in contact with know what you do for a living. Wear a catchy pin showing a house, or a necktie that is decorated with houses. People love to talk about real estate. When they know you are a real estate agent, they will want to pick your brain about the market.

Once, on a return trip from a vacation in Florida, I sat next to an older lady on the plane. She noticed the pin I was wearing. I call it my "travel pin" because I wear it every time I travel. The pin is shiny rhinestones and in the shape of a "For Sale" sign and says "SOLD."

We started a conversation that lasted 2 hours. She told me she was moving back up North to live with her son. She had a luxury home on the Intracoastal Waterway that she would be selling. She asked me if I could help her with the sale. I told her I was not licensed to do business in Florida, however, I could help her through our relocation network. She was thrilled to have someone she knew who could help her. I contacted an agent in Florida the next day who was delighted to receive the referral and sold the house for $937,000. The referral fee to me more than paid for my Florida vacation... and ... *I was able to help someone.*

Be in contact with your sphere of influence on a regular basis. These are people you know: friends, relatives, neighbors, clergy, people on the street, and people in social organizations. You are open for business every day as a real estate agent. This means you must talk to these people and let them know what you do for a living.

You can never assume that people know what you are doing. It can cost you money in your pocket if people do not know what you do, and therefore do not use your services. Do not be shy. Offer to help. Who better than YOU to help them buy or sell real estate?!

Working with the Buyers

"I have more fun and enjoy more financial success
when I stop trying to get what I want and start
helping other people get what they want."
- Spencer Johnson, *One Minute Salesperson*

It is true that I closed over 100 transactions annually, but remember I never really *sold* a home. People *buy* homes with our help and guidance. Agents provide the service and skillfully coordinate the process. Really, what we do is to...

HELP PEOPLE MAKE GOOD
BUSINESS DECISIONS

Don't try to SELL anyone a home! They will sense your misguided objective and run like crazy. I have gotten more business from people who came to me after having had a bad experience with another agent who was "trying to sell them a home." In every sale there is a *person*. Live and work using the Golden Rule – "Do unto others as you would have them do unto you."

Set the stage at your first personal meeting with the buyer. Start your business relationship off on the right foot. Take control from the beginning and meet with prospects on your terms. By this I mean, *schedule an appointment*. Meet in your office or a public place like a coffee shop. If they are unwilling to meet on your terms, they probably are not serious buyers. Conduct your business like other professionals.

Once the customer/client is in your office, you start with a buyer counseling session. This is the "getting to know you" time.

Ask questions. Find out their motivation for looking. Ask if they have a home now or if they are renting. If they are renting, find out if they are on a lease. (If they're on a lease, they may not be able to purchase until the lease has ended.) Discuss financing, insurance, home inspections and the entire purchase process from start to close.

If you practice in a state where buyer agency is law, explain in detail the benefits of working with you. Tell the buyer about– **O.L.D. C.A.R.** This is an acronym for your responsibilities as a buyer's agent. It stands for:

OBEDIENCE

LAWFUL INSTRUCTION

DISCLOSURE

CONFIDENTIALITY

ACCOUNTABILITY

REASONABLE SKILL AND CARE

Be sure to LISTEN and LEARN during this question and answer session to discover what the buyer wants from you and a new home.

Ask them what their expectations are from you. I'll bet no other agent has ever asked this question.

Have them write on paper a list of everything they WISH TO GET IN THE NEW HOME. For example:

- Location
- Price
- Style
- Square footage
- Number of bedrooms
- Number of bathrooms
- Garage
- Age
- Property size
- Other

When you do your "homework" properly, everyone benefits. The benefit of taking the time to analyze the buyer's needs and wants, is that you will eliminate wasting time showing properties they aren't even interested in.

I question the agents who tell me they've shown dozens of homes to a buyer who has yet to purchase a home. It should not be necessary to show 50 homes to one buyer if you have taken the time to fully communicate with the buyer during the buyer counseling session. In other words, listen to what their needs and wants are and you'll be able to narrow down the home search.

You can run ragged if you don't have direction. You will need to exercise your sales skills and use closing techniques to help them find their ideal home. A great technique I use is, after showing a few homes, I will use this dialogue:

"Now that I've shown you a few homes, if you hypothetically had to select one...which home would it be?"

You are not telling the buyer they MUST select one of the homes they just saw, but you are eliminating the ones they absolutely do not want. This gets them in the mindset of choosing one over the other. It also starts them thinking about moving into a new home.

Most Top Producers polled say they show about 10 homes before the buyer finds the perfect one for them.

Now, we all have a story about showing a lot of homes to one buyer. I have one, too. The above is an ideal way to go about things, but not always a perfect science. The most homes I ever showed to one family in my entire career was 24. These buyers were referred to me through our relocation department and were supposedly pre-screened. I was told they wanted a cookie cutter, 3-bedroom, 2-bath home. They had to buy over the weekend and I located 24 homes that I hoped would fit the bill.

They were looking for a 3-bedroom, 2-bath home, but they wanted something unique. They were Mormons who required a farmhouse type home with a brook or some running water on the property. They would be having gardens for their food. We finally found their perfect home, but it was only when I completely understood what they really were looking for.

When you are working with a buyer and going to be showing homes, there are some important guidelines to follow.

Drive a 4-door car for the comfort of your passengers, and so everyone can get in and out of the car easily. Travel in one car, with you as the driver. If your customers/clients bring kids or animals, you can go along in their car with them.

Keep your car neat and clean at all times. It's your office on wheels and a reflection of you. Remove all the old empty coffee cups and leftover french fries, and brush off any animal hair. Get your car washed if it is dirty. You would be surprised how many agents aren't aware of the consequences of "little things" like having a clean car.

I recall a situation when a particular wealthy buyer was assigned to an experienced agent in my office. The agent thought she had built a good rapport with this person. After touring the area and viewing several homes, they returned to the office to schedule a follow-up appointment to continue the search.

Much to the surprise of the agent, the buyer turned to the office manager, requesting to be reassigned to someone else. She said it was not personal, but she couldn't stand riding in a car that was dirty, full of dog smell and dog hair. That agent lost a good piece of business because of a dirty car.

Every trade has its tricks. I want to share with you a couple of pointers that could make your showing more appealing to the buyer.

Always be enthusiastic about the showings. Highlight the positive aspects of the interior and exterior of the property. Try to avoid adding your personal opinion of any aspects of the home. If they like something, you should too.

Walk into the room first and go to the furthest end of the room first. It will make the living space look larger. When entering different rooms, proper use of words can help. For example, instead of "This is the kitchen" say, "This is YOUR kitchen."

Save time in many different ways. If you do go into a home that the buyer clearly does not like, there is no reason to force them to stay. Move onto the next home. Remember, you are not the buyer, you are the agent helping them make a good decision. It is not your place to impose your likes and dislikes.

Also, if you pull up in front of a house and the buyers immediately say they don't want to see it, respect their wishes. Call the homeowner and cancel your showing, and go on to the next property.

In order to help your buyer find their perfect home, you must continually ask them, "What did you like/dislike about this property?" You need ongoing attempts to tie them down.

Working with the Sellers

"Get out of your comfort zone." - Mary Kay

REALTORS® DON'T GROW OLD... THEY JUST GROW LISTLESS

Early in my career, I thought I would concentrate my efforts on working with buyers. I imagined that working with buyers would be less stressful and more exciting. I quickly divided my efforts between servicing buyers and finding those listings. Ultimately, I became a very strong listing agent.

It wasn't long before I noticed the most successful agents were the strong listing agents. Listings **are** the backbone of the business in any market. Listings will make your office phone ring and attract buyers. Listings are an opportunity to get your name in an advertisement. This is the kind of exposure you want to build your business.

When you are a listing agent you have a written employment contract and you are really in business. You don't have to be glued to a desk to accomplish your job. You have some flexibility. You can negotiate a transaction from just about anywhere. I have successfully negotiated many of my listings while vacationing on a tropical beach, when traveling in a car across the desert, and even from the deck of a luxury cruise ship, just to mention a few fun places that were far from my desk in the office.

There are listing opportunities everywhere. This goes back to sales, don't be a Secret Agent! Be alert. You never know when someone will enter into your life needing your help to sell their home.

Once, while taking my morning walk, I noticed an old man who was retrieving letters from his mailbox. He dropped a few envelopes. It was obvious he was having a tough time bending down. I went over to help him pick up the letters.

His excitement was apparent when he opened a letter from an assisted living home. We began chatting and he told me that this letter was his acceptance for residency. He went on to say he would be selling his house and moving to a "quieter place." My antenna is always up, so I asked if he had a real estate agent in mind to help him market his home for sale. When he said no, I quickly offered my services and got the listing!

The million dollar question is, *Where are all the listings?*

The million dollar answer is, *They are everywhere!*

True, the listings are everywhere, and it's your work to find them through proven techniques.

The following are avenues to the listings:

- FARMING
- FOR SALE BY OWNER
- EXPIRED LISTINGS
- PUBLIC OPEN HOUSE

Each of these avenues has a systematic process to be effective.

Farming is cultivating. The dictionary says to cultivate means to foster growth. I guess this is why we've adopted the word FARM in our business. We are fostering growth.

Effective farming means getting to know an area and the people who live there. You will become the expert in your "farm" and be known as an expert by everyone who lives in your "farm."

The most logical area to start is your immediate neighborhood. Let everyone around you know what you do for a living.

The "farming" system includes mailing, warm calling, personal visiting and follow-up.

Send handwritten notes to introduce yourself. Let them know you are their "neighborhood REALTOR®." After a few days place warm calls to follow up the mailing. Next comes the personal visit. This means... knock on doors!

The door knocking is a real step out of the box for many agents. I wouldn't have you doing this if it didn't have a BIG return for your efforts! Just think, not only will you be working, but you will actually get to know your neighbors and some other folks in your town. You will be remembered.

You want to be the only person someone thinks of when it comes to real estate. When was the last time an agent knocked on your door? I'll bet the answer is never.

Think of how you would feel if you woke up one day to see a "For Sale" sign in your neighbor's yard with the name of another agent and not yours? Then you find out the neighbor didn't know you were in real estate. There's no one to blame but you for not getting that listing.

When you go door knocking, have your business cards and a little gift for them to remember you. In the fall, I deliver small pumpkins to my "farm." I stick my business card on the pumpkin and leave it near the front door if the owners are out.

Around national holidays like Memorial Day, Flag Day and The 4th of July, I place the American flag with my business card on it in the yards of my "farm."

I admit it was hard for me at first to do the door knocking thing. But it became easier as time passed and soon I found it fun. Over the years, people started looking for me to show up with my token gift and to talk about the market. The listings followed! I would love driving through my farm areas and seeing my "For Sale" signs everywhere. The houses sold with my help.

PUBLIC OPEN HOUSE

Another great avenue for listings and buyers are the Public Open House. These folks are your "WALK-INS."

Public Open Houses were designed by real estate agents years ago to attract prospects, both buyers and sellers.

I've secured many listings as a result of the POH. The neighbors wander over to check out a house because they are getting ready to sell themselves. People show up who are starting their home search and have yet to list their home.

There is a systematic procedure in effectively hosting a Public Open House. Follow these simple guidelines.

- Advertise in your local paper or online with an address and price.
- Mail and/or call neighbors to invite them to the Open House.
- Place Open House signs on the property one week prior to the Open House.
- Wear your name tag – I know this sounds basic, but so many agents do not do this.
- Stage the home – turn on lights and open blinds for maximum lighting.
- Turn on some soft background music and put around some light air freshener to delight the senses. (A great tip is to use a little cinnamon and cloves in a pot of water on the stove, simmering. It smells great.)
- Place business cards throughout the house on side tables and countertops.
- Have a sign-in sheet or guest book with a few fake names already written in. No one wants to be the first name but you will need this information in order to follow up.

- Have shoe covers available or ask prospects to remove their shoes "per the owner's request." Shoe covers will keep the floor clean. The homeowners are impressed that I have respect for the house, and prospective buyers want to work with me because they will realize I respect other people's properties as well. They knew I would treat them the same. Treat this home as you would your own.

- **This is the most important tip.** Escort visitors through the home <u>individually</u>.

    - Have other prospects wait outside and put a sign on the door when you are showing the home. If they are serious buyers, they will wait.
    - Give any prospect that cannot wait the option of a private showing at a later time.
    - This will give you an opportunity to build rapport.

- Be sure to ask all prospects if they are working with another agent. If these people are buyers and your state has buyer agency by law, ask if they have a written buyer agency with that agent.

When the Open House is over, send handwritten "Thank you for attending my Open House" notes to prospects who visited. Do this immediately.

Sample Follow-up Note:

Dear Mr. and Mrs. Buyer,

I wanted to thank you for stopping by my listing at 10 Main Street, Anywhere, USA on Sunday, [month] [day], [year].

If you would like any further information regarding this listing, or information on any other available properties in your price range, please contact me. I would be happy to help you with any of your home buying needs.

I can be reached by phone at: 444-555-1234 or via email: myname@ email.com. Have a great day.

Sincerely,
My Name
Company Name
Company Address
Phone Numbers/Email

(MINIMUM OF TWO BUSINESS CARDS ENCLOSED.)

Follow up, follow up, and follow up again.

Later in the week, call the prospects to ask if they received your note. At this time you will ask if they have questions about the house they visited and/or if they would like to see other homes. Now you are having a conversation with them and it's time to suggest setting an appointment so you can further help them.

This system for hosting a Public Open House really works. I hosted a Public Open House every Sunday consecutively for the first 9 months of my career. My business exploded! Make this a part of your weekly plan and your business will grow, too.

I got my first buyer from a Public Open House. It was the Sunday of Thanksgiving weekend. Some of my associates were negative, and one "experienced" agent even told me it was a bad idea to schedule an Open House on that day. They said no one would come since it was a holiday weekend.

The property was a townhouse in a lovely condominium complex. The owners were out of town. I offered a raffle prize to visitors. As it turned out, I actually had a surprising number of visiting prospects. It seemed people were looking for something to do and I was the only Open House in town.

I added 9 prospects to my business base that day. It gets better... One of the prospects was visiting family who lived in that very complex. They had been thinking of relocating closer to their grown kids and grandchildren, as they had recently sold their home in Virginia. They loved the townhouse. We wrote up their Offer to Purchase that night and it was accepted by the sellers that evening. The unit sold for $210,000. My fee for service was in excess of $3,000. I'd say that was a good day's pay for working the Sunday of a holiday!

Now don't get me wrong, there were many other times when no one has shown up to my Open Houses. Those are the days I use to review my business plan. I write notes to prospects or past clients. I even enjoyed the blessing of having some quiet time. I remained focused and didn't allow those times to discourage me.

When you view every opportunity as a chance to build your business, success is yours.

•••

EXPIRED LISTINGS
OPEN MORE DOORS TO WEALTH

Oxygen, please…CPR for expired listings needed…breathe some "fresh air" into the expired listings and make money.

Expired listings require immediate response and a lot of diplomacy. These prospective clients come along with their own set of challenges that an agent must anticipate. For example, the Expireds are angry because they have been on the market for months. Despite market conditions of any sort, if the house has not sold they blame their agent. They are already disgruntled and discouraged.

It's important to act quickly with expired listings because other agents are calling them, too. Be sure to cross-reference the expired listings with the New-to-Market listings before any contact. Oftentimes, they will re-list with their present agent. If you call them before checking the status, you will not only look foolish, but you are in danger of crossing agency boundaries.

It is important to be prepared with a dialogue that makes sense. Whatever you do, do not call and tell them, "I have a buyer for your house." They will only shout back at you by asking, "If you had a buyer for my house, then where the heck were you when I was on the market?"

Instead, simply call them and say, "I see your house is off the market. Are you still interested in selling?" Do not say any more until they answer.

If the answer is NO, and they no longer want to sell, then let it go. Mail a follow-up note wishing them well and add them to your contact list. They will probably sell in the future and you want to be the first to know when they are ready.

If they say YES, then start a dialogue. . . Ask to schedule a time to come over and view the house. Treat this like any other listing opportunity and start from scratch. Show interest, concern, take notes, build rapport and most importantly...listen to them!

Whatever you do, be careful not to criticize anything about the prior agent. Do not comment on what the other agent could have or should have done better. When we put down others, we put down ourselves too. Schedule another appointment with all the decision-makers (all owners) of the property present to review your market analysis. Try to find out what they did not like about the other agent. You will need to offer a better, more powerful plan of action in order to secure the listing!

When you bring the Expireds back to life, you will bring your business to the next level.

•••

FOR SALE BY OWNER (F.S.B.O)

FSBO is a great way to find listings. These people need your help!

I get a kick out of the FSBO. These are the few who believe that just because they've lived in a home they know everything about marketing and merchandising that home for sale and that they are real estate agents simply by association. So does this mean that just because they've lived in their body for a certain number of years they are a doctor by association? The answer is no.

When I was a new agent I was told there were a lot of opportunities in FSBOs. I was instructed to call them and offer my services. I remember it like yesterday the first FSBO I called. I didn't have a scripted dialogue, but I thought if I was nice and polite and offered my help I would win them over. Not so.

My first FSBO call was almost my last! The person I called shouted all sorts of profanities at me and told me she hated real estate agents. She said she could sell the house herself and that I was never to call her again. The truth is I was scared to death and never wanted to call another FSBO again.

I learned that the FSBO sellers are usually nice people who are angry because they are frustrated. Sometimes these people have had a bad experience with an agent and feel we are all the same. Despite their situation, the fact remains that they really do need our help. Whenever I see a "For Sale By Owner" yard sign, my brain immediately transposes those FSBO letters into H E L P.

According to the National Association of REALTORS® (NAR), the number one reason FSBOs don't want to use a real estate agent is because they don't want to pay the commission. The fact of the matter is, according to NAR statistics, homes that were sold using a real estate agent netted the sellers much more than those sold by a FSBO. It doesn't make sense or dollars for people not to hire a real estate agent. It's important that we share this factual information with the public.

The FSBO sellers are easy to find. Look for yard signs, classified ads in the newspaper, and online sites. Do not let the 'NO BROKERS' on the ads scare you away. These properties are public offerings and you are one of the public.

Your initial contact with the FSBO can be a simple handwritten letter. Let them know who you are and wish them well with the efforts to sell.

Wait a few days, then make a warm call just asking if they received your note and if they have any questions about the market.

Tell them you would like to hand-deliver a gift that will help them sell the house faster. It's my FSBO FIRST AID KIT. You can email me for a FREE download of this useful tool.

This FSBO FIRST AID KIT is a package full of information the seller might need for the home sale. It's a large pile of paperwork that oftentimes shocks the seller into a better understanding of all the work an agent does to sell a house.

Call the FSBO using the following dialogue:

"Hello. My name is Jane Doe from ABC Realty and I am NOT calling to list your house. Because you live in a neighborhood where I DO sell homes, I would like to come over to preview your house for a possible buyer. I also have a little something that may help you during the selling process."

The key words in this dialogue are possible buyer. You are not saying you have a buyer now. You may have a buyer in the future so the dialogue is not false. In any event, this dialogue works into a face-to-face meeting with the seller. You also want to preview every home in your selling area and need to know what this home looks like on the inside.

Make an appointment to meet with the FSBO as soon as possible. Hand-deliver the FSBO FIRST AID KIT and ask permission to check back with them in a week or so for an update on their progress. Very often they will have nothing to report and this will give you an opportunity to offer your professional marketing services.

There is a wealth of business waiting for you with the FSBOs. Don't be afraid to work this resource. If you need a boost to get you going, read the book *Feel the Fear, and Do It Anyway* by Susan Jeffers, Ph.D. Her book offers dynamic techniques for turning fear into power and action. Try to contact at least one "For Sale By Owner" each day and watch your business grow.

THE MARKET ANALYSIS
(Broker's Price Opinion/Competitive Market Analysis)

The value of a home is one of the BIGGEST concerns for every seller. I'd say this is one of the main reasons people call our offices. They want to pick our brains.

Let the sellers know that to complete an accurate opinion of value it requires knowledge and experience, and it takes time. I tell the seller it takes me about 6-8 hours to compile the information on value.

A big mistake agents make is to tell people, "With the computer programs, I can whip up a CMA in no time." Keep track of the time spent after the initial call for a CMA and you'll get the picture. The computer does supply information that will streamline the CMA, but it's not a substitute for doing your homework altogether.

You cannot rely completely on the computer to provide accurate information. It's not always up-to-date. You must physically go to your local town hall or county seat.

Property research should be done in the Assessor's office then continue to the Town Clerk's office. Read over the deed and know the names of all the legal owners. Look for liens and check to see if the mortgage is clear. You need to know if the home you are potentially going to list is even sellable.

In light of the current market and in any market, you need to know if there is enough money to cover the mortgage pay off, any liens, etc., and your commission! And you DO want to get paid, don't you?

I stress the importance of doing your own research. You cannot rely completely on technology to do your job. Let me share with you a real-life situation that happened to me just now while I was writing this book.

A long time ago, I had set a goal to own another home near the ocean. I spent months with a full-time REALTOR® looking for my dream home. When I finally found that perfect place, I made an offer. The offer was negotiated, came to acceptance and went directly to contract. Then there was a 3-day attorney review before the contract would be valid.

In the meantime, I told my family about the house purchase and they started making travel plans for summer vacation at the shore. A week passed and I called my agent questioning why I hadn't heard anything. I was then told that there was a "silent partner." When I asked if this silent partner was on the deed, I was told by my agent that she did not know, but she would check with the listing agent who was a top producer.

The listing agent said she only remembered one owner when she sold the house and there was only one person at the closing. Furthermore, she stated that her online research of the property showed only one owner. She never physically went to the Town Hall. I wasn't satisfied with this answer so I called the Town Hall myself. I spoke with the town Assessor and learned, within minutes, that there were TWO OWNERS ON THE DEED! I Googled the owners and learned they lived out of state. Then I found their phone numbers through the internet and called both owners.

This is when I learned that the silent partner/owner who lived in another state knew nothing about his house being listed. This same "silent partner" had no intention of selling. By the way, this home had been on the market for over 9 months as an illegal listing. It was advertised to the hilt for all that time at a large expense to the broker.

As for me, I was heartbroken that the home I was all set to move into was not really ever for sale.

Then one of my daughters said to me, "And you wonder why people don't like real estate agents!" We live in a very litigious society and this very situation could easily have become a lawsuit against the listing agent and I, as a buyer, would likely have won punitive damages.

I suppose this happened to me so I could have a true-life story to share with you and encourage you to go all the way when it comes to doing your homework on listings. The simple solution to a potential tragedy is to do your homework!

Once you have all of the information for a complete CMA, it's on to the job interview. I suggest using the 2-step approach when interviewing for the job. The first step is to meet the owners and start building a rapport. Show up on time for your appointment. Use a notepad to take notes. I've had more sellers comment on my note-taking, saying other agents were not that detailed. Take room measurements and have them help you. Don't shortcut. It won't pay.

If sellers ask your advice on what may be needed to prepare the home for sale, tell them, "Staging is a client service and I'll be happy to address that, should you hire me to market your house."

If they ask for a "ballpark" price, let them know that would be a PFA number. When they ask what PFA means, tell them PLUCKED FROM AIR.

Don't make the mistake of giving them any inkling of a price opinion because whatever it is will get stuck in their mind. If it's too low they might ask you not to come back. If it's too high, they might hold you to it.

Step 2 is to schedule a meeting with ALL of the owners/decision-makers. If you cannot meet with ALL at the same time, you may be wasting your time.

Most interviews are conducted in the seller's home. It would be best if you can get the owners into your office since the atmosphere is more professional than in their home. When meeting in their home, sit at a table rather than in the living room. This gives you more control of the interview. Do not review your CMA or discuss the house value until you have SOLD YOUR COMPANY AND SOLD YOURSELF. Be prepared with a well-organized listing presentation book.

Prepare, Practice and Perform

Your presentation book should be kept to approximately 20 pages. Try to stay continuous with landscape or portrait pictures so that you are not moving your book sideways and upright. Your presentation book should include, but is not limited to, the following items:

- **Emphasize Credentials**
  - Copy of your Real Estate License
  - Your Personal Resume
  - Code of Ethics
  - Certificates and designations
  - Civic or community involvement
  - Testimonials from past clients

• Sell Your Company

- Company information – how many offices, agents, local owners?
- Relocation information – makes you GLOBAL, brings buyers, you can offer outgoing referrals.
- Company and relocation websites, if applicable.
- Samples of customized flyers or ads for the subject property.
- Advertising venues – i.e., newspapers, magazines, websites, etc.
- Listing Agreement Form

You can build your value by letting them know your FULL Job Description, or as I like to call it your Marketing and Merchandising Strategies. An incomplete list follows – feel free to add your own.

Marketing and Merchandising Strategies / Job Description - Initial Activities

- Establish pricing and positioning in the marketplace.
- Provide pre-marketing assistance – staging your home for the marketplace.
- List on the Multiple Listing Service.
- Provide you with a copy of the MLS computerized printout for your approval.
- List property on the internet.
- Install key box – where applicable (explain how these are an added security feature.)
- Take photographs for advertising and brochures.
- Order property sign.
- Schedule initial local display advertisement.

- Familiarize my office agents at sales meetings and preview the property.
- Schedule and arrange Broker Open House with incentives.
- Schedule Public Open House.
- Network properties to all of our offices.
- Schedule Direct Mail Marketing Program.
- Create a "Media Center" in your home that will include the Home Book, property brochures, sign-in sheets, mortgage information, the National School Report, etc.
- Place "Special Feature" cards on the property, highlighting the assets of your home.
- Follow up on all property showings and provide you with feedback.
- Advertise your property on a rotational basis.
- Review advertising responses.
- Schedule additional Open Houses as appropriate.
- Update ad copy and photos as needed.
- Evaluate feedback regularly and adjust pricing.
- Review activity on comparable properties.
- Continue to promote property to Multiple Listing Service members.
- Provide updated information and promote property at branch office meetings.

Job Description – Ongoing Activities

- Provide you with monthly reports, including property activity, updated market data and pricing recommendations.
- Pre-qualify prospective buyers or direct to local banker.
- Present all Offers to Purchase in a timely manner.
- Negotiate effectively to obtain the highest price in the least amount of time when an offer is received.

- Provide you with lists of service providers, such as attorneys, inspectors, environmental specialists, lenders, insurance companies, and movers.
- Coordinate building inspections.
- Make certain that contingency dates are met on schedule (mortgage, building inspection, etc.)

Job Description – At Closing

- Schedule a final walk-through of your property.
- Arrange to remove the "For Sale" sign and lock box (if applicable.)
- Communicate with attorneys and bankers to ensure a smooth closing.
- Check to make sure both parties have transferred all utilities. (I will provide assistance, although it is your responsibility to make the necessary calls.)
- Attend the closing or have a company representative attend.

AT ALL TIMES:

PROVIDE YOU WITH "SUPERIOR SERVICE!"

Begin your time together asking the seller, "What are your expectations of me?"

Another great dialogue to break the ice is: *"I'm not here to list your home, rather I'm here to share my marketing and merchandising strategies in the hopes of being hired for a job."*

When conducting your interview you need to be prepared to answer these common questions:

- Why should they hire your company? What is unique about your company?

- How is your company different from the competition?

- What is today's market like? What is the average time on the market?

- Is it a good time to buy? Why?

- Is it a good time to sell? Why?

- What makes you the BEST real estate agent?

- What makes you unique?

Be careful to avoid criticizing the competition. Spend time boosting your company and you. Discuss their motivation for selling – are they eager to move for a job or schools, or do they not have a deadline? Also, ask them about prior experiences with other agents. This can help you determine what they liked or did not like. Try to avoid doing the same thing.

In closing, and prior to reviewing the CMA, use this dialogue to close "the deal":

"Now that I've shared with you about my company and myself, don't you agree I would be the right agent to market your house for sale?"

When you are ready to discuss the CMA, go over the details entirely. Do not just give the price. Start by having the seller write down the price they believe the house is worth on a piece of paper. Tell them not to reveal it to you until you've given your price opinion. Or have them show it to you so you know what you're working with.

Discuss with the seller what the difference between asking price and sold price is. Asking price is a fake number which does not become real until someone brings money to the table. In many markets nationwide, homes sell within 3%-5% of the asking price. This means when you get the price to where the market is, the home is likely to sell.

Let the seller know that ultimately THEY set the asking price. You can give them opinions but the number is up to them. Then it is up to you whether you want to take the listing, especially if they want to severely overprice.

Explain the dangers of overpricing. When you overprice the market you often end up chasing the market. You can use this dialogue, "Do you want to bet on the market or net IN the market?"

Show them a price range based on the information you came up with. If you decide on a number that is way below what they believe the house is worth, you again need to decide if this is a listing you want to take. You might spend a lot of energy on an overpriced listing for another agent to come along once it expires and sell the house instead of you.

When giving them this range it is important to educate sellers as to how you determine the price range that you come up with. Explain how you come up with the price:

- Comparables of Sold Properties no more than 6 months old.
- Comparables of recent Pending Properties.
- Competitive Active Listings.
- Adjusting prices according to the property – bedrooms, bathrooms, garage, size, etc.
- Dealing with a changing real estate market.

Refer to the Code of Ethics and Standards of Practice 1-3 which states, "REALTORS®, in attempting to secure a listing, shall not deliberately mislead the owner as to market value." After you explain in detail the CMA and discuss your fee, then close again by saying:

"Don't hire an agent based on the PRICE they give you or the COMMISSION they charge. Rather, you should hire an agent based on:

> **#1 their honesty and integrity**
> **#2 their knowledge of the marketplace**
> **#3 their ability to get the job done!"**

Say no more. Wait for their response.

You can also use a written guarantee to secure the listing. A written guarantee sample is below.

- I will provide you with a complete professional Market Analysis of your property.
- I will enter into a TEAM relationship with you that will remain as such throughout the term of the listing agreement.
- I will keep our conversations confidential.
- I will give you professional advice on how to enhance your house for sale.
- I will enter your listing into the Multiple Listing Service (MLS) within 24 hours of signing an agreement with my company.
- I will place a lock box on your property with your permission within 24 hours of signing an agreement with my company (where applicable.)
- I will order a "For Sale" sign to be placed on your property (where allowed.)
- I will prepare a new listing packet to include a school report, area information and a sign in sheet.

- I will return all calls from you as quickly as possible.
- I will present all offers to you up until closing.
- I will use professional and diligent efforts to obtain the highest and best price for your property.
- I will communicate feedback to you regarding showings as soon as I receive that information from showing agents.
- I will hold Public Open Houses at your convenience.
- I will negotiate on your behalf and in your best interest.
- I will act as the transaction coordinator through to closing.
- I will attend the closing or have a company representative attend the closing.

_____   _____
REALTOR® SIGNATURE   SELLER SIGNATURE

•••

Before leaving your home, VISUALIZE that you WILL get the job and WILL walk away with a signed listing agreement, at your fee, with your recommended price, and for your suggested length of time.

Picture a "For Sale" sign with your name on it in front on the house.

Remind yourself that you are the BEST person to market the home for sale and you will get the listing!

Now that you've secured the listing…it's time for:

STAGING A HOME FOR SALE

Staging Matters!

SIGHT…SOUND…SMELL

I learned early in my career that proper staging usually makes a house sell faster and for more money. Because most home buying decisions are based on emotion, we need to prepare the home so that it appeals to the emotions of the buyers. By this I mean, the house must **LOOK** *light, bright and clutter-free,* **SOUND** *peaceful, and* **SMELL** *appealing.*

Please note that I do not suggest giving any staging advice to a seller until you have been HIRED by them to market the house. The reason for keeping quiet until you have the listing is twofold. First, as I said earlier, any advice on staging a home (as far as I am concerned) is considered a "client service." Until someone becomes a client, they are not privy to this service. Second, there can be danger in being truthful because the truth could hurt someone's feelings. They may love the bright yellow shag carpeting. If you suggest carpet replacement before you secure the listing you could potentially insult the seller and NEVER get the listing. Use your diplomacy and please think before you speak.

Let the seller know that a part of your marketing strategy is to review preparing the home for sale. I tell them, *"The way you live in a home and the way you prepare a home for sale are two different things."* I first heard this quote from Barb Schwarz who is nationally known as a pioneer for home staging. That was over 20 years ago and I have been using the same line to sellers ever since then. Barb is one of my favorite trainers when it comes to staging a home. She is a fountain of knowledge and I suggest checking her programs out online.

We start staging suggestions by telling the seller to depersonalize. Let your clients know that they should remove all personal photos from the house and get rid of as much clutter as possible. In fact, it's a great idea to start moving non-essential items out of the home.

When I show a home and walk into a kitchen with a refrigerator full of magnets and kids' posters, the countertop piled high with papers and junk, the trash can full of smelly garbage and the litter box that hasn't been cleaned in days, I do not blame the seller. I blame the listing agent for not educating the seller on how to prepare their home for sale. It is the listing agent's responsibility to go room by room offering staging instructions.

Something else I recommend, if you are not already there, is to learn about the power of Feng Shui.

A good friend of mine, Holly Ziegler, has written two books on this subject. Her books are *Sell Your Home FASTER With Feng Shui* and *Buy Your Home SMARTER with Feng Shui*. Holly's advice is invaluable and her books are great gifts for sellers and buyers alike and will help you and your clients to understand how Feng Shui affects the home sale and purchase. There are many buyers who will only buy a home if the Feng Shui is right.

You can only make a first impression once. This also applies when showing off a home for sale. These are a few of the most commonly overlooked enhancements that, when addressed, can attract a buyer.

Exterior Home Staging Necessities Include:

• Mailbox and post standing straight, painted, and like new
• Front door painted if needed
• Working doorbell
• Lawn mowed
• Seasonal flowers planted and landscaping mulch added

Interior Home Staging Necessities Include:

- Depersonalize by removing all family photos.
- Kitchen countertops are to be cleared of all clutter. Only appliances that are used every day should be on the counter. Everything else should be put away.
- Refrigerator should be free of magnets or posters and looking new and clean.
- Trash cans should be emptied of smelly garbage.
- Cat litter and animal waste should always be removed quickly.
- No dishes should be left in the sink or in the drying rack.
- Lights should be left on in all rooms during showings. Blinds should also be open to let in natural light.
- Have soft background music playing when showing.
- Place air fresheners where needed.
- Beds should be made and laundry should be put away.
- Vacuum regularly.

These small tasks are proven to bring large rewards.

Here is a little example of how staging works to sell a home. I had a beautiful home in a beautiful neighborhood. I had a person interested, but as soon as we opened the door we were greeted by a little dog that did nothing but bark. Even though the dog was caged, the buyer didn't want to go in. I called the listing agent and asked if she'd be able to remove the dog for a little while and put some air freshener around to cover any dog smell. The seller did this and subsequently the buyer ended up putting in an offer that was later accepted.

A home that is staged will show beautifully and "hug" them when they come in to make them want to stay. This will not always sell the home to the first buyer that comes in, but they will have a positive experience. A home that shows well, sells well.

Powerful Phone, Text and Email Techniques

"Before everything else, getting ready is the secret of success." - Henry Ford

Open this door and begin.......

$$$ DIALING FOR DOLLARS $$$

You can only make a first impression once.

When you answer the phone, you'd better give your best shot to make something happen!

The proper use of language and words can mean the difference between gaining a client or losing one. A caller will not always hear what we say, but they will be aware of tonality and response. They are more likely to react positively if your conversation sounds like you really care about them.

Be ever mindful of the words you use. Words must be used correctly to be effective or they can be damaging.

I have rephrased an old saying that goes:

STICKS AND STONES
WILL BREAK YOUR BONES AND
NAMES WILL NEVER HURT YOU.

The truth is:

STICKS AND STONES
WILL BREAK YOUR BONES AND
NAMES WILL ***EVER*** HURT YOU.

Just think about something nasty someone may have said to you over the years. I'll bet it took a long time to forget what was said. In fact, maybe you are still carrying that hurt today.

If you have any doubt about the power of words, I suggest reading *The Hidden Messages in Water* by Dr. Masaru Emoto, an internationally renowned Japanese scientist. Dr. Emoto discovered that molecules of water are affected by our thoughts, words and feelings. His studies are remarkable and show how the human body is affected by words since the human body is made up largely of water.

THINK BEFORE YOU SPEAK!

Modify your vocabulary to create a smooth and winning delivery. This will elevate your level of professionalism when communicating with others. The proper use of words makes a

BIG DIFFERENCE.

Work on modifying your professional vocabulary. Below are some common words that, when modified, sound more professional as well as elevating us above the rest.

COMMON	MODIFIED
• Deal	• Transaction
• Commission	• Fee for service
• Listing Presentation	• Job Interview
• How much do you want to spend?	• Where is your buying power?
• Price	• Total investment
• Down Payment	• Initial investment
• Sign	• Authorize, Approve
• Contract	• Agreement
• Buy	• Own
• House	• Moves client out
• Home	• Moves client in
• When do you want to buy a house?	• How soon do you want to be in your new home?
• Schedule an appointment	• Let's get together
• Price reduction	• Reposition in the marketplace

Tonality is easy to address if you simply remember to:

SMILE BEFORE YOU DIAL

Keep the smile on throughout your call and it will be "heard"!

Think dollars $$$ EVERY TIME the phone rings and EVERY TIME you receive an email with an inquiry about real estate!

The ONLY reason an agent should be taking floor time or returning emails is to:

SCHEDULE AN APPOINTMENT

One of the biggest complaints I hear from brokers and managers is that their agents are not converting the call-ins or emails to appointments.

A scenario of how most duty calls are answered goes like this: The office phone rings. A caller asks questions about a listing. The duty agent proceeds to give away every piece of information the caller asks for. Within minutes, the agent is sitting there holding a phone with a dial tone because the caller got what they wanted and hung up. The agent is left with no information on this call-in and no way to reach that person again.

This is usually when the agent moans and says something like, "There's no business out there. It's just another nosy neighbor calling in. Just my bad luck."

According to national statistics, 97% of the people in this country who pick up the phone to get information on ANYTHING that is for sale are serious buyers.

Remember this statistic the next time you are answering phones, and be armed with a powerful dialogue to get what you need from the caller to **schedule an appointment.**

Oh, by the way, if the caller really was a nosy neighbor, I've got news for you, nosy neighbors buy/sell too. As I mentioned previously, start observing neighborhoods and notice when one "For Sale" sign goes up. Often within days or weeks another "For Sale" sign will appear. Have you ever heard of the Joneses? Well, people like keeping up with the Joneses!

If you're wondering about email inquiries on listings, according to NAR statistics, nearly all homebuyers start their home search on the internet. These people ARE serious. The majority of them use an agent!

So my question is, "Why do we react as we do in our business? Why are we still 'jumping'?"

Convey compassion to everyone. Whether it's a phone call, email or face to face, let people know you want to care for them. The public is sometimes afraid of the agent because of preconceived notions that the agent is a scoundrel. I think some see us as vultures ready to pounce on the prey.

In fact, the agents are usually very good professionals who want to help. People will care to work with us when we show that we care for them.

Do you want to be a switchboard operator giving out information all day to strangers? I hope there is a method to this madness and I hope it is to convert the caller into a client.

A good dialogue will enable you to convert the call-ins and emails into appointments. There are key questions that need to be answered, but you must be tactful when asking them.

You want to enter into a caring and casual conversation with the caller to accomplish your goal of scheduling the appointment.

Here's a checklist of what we need from the caller:

- **The caller's name**
- **The caller's address**
- **The caller's phone numbers**
- **The caller's email address**
- **Are they working with another REALTOR®? If so, do they have a buyer's agency with that agent?**
- **What's their motivation?**

Now:

SCHEDULE AN APPOINTMENT

It may sound easy, but you need to have a plan to make the dialogue work.

Prepare, Practice and Perform! The 3 P's work.

Your brain has to function like a director. You are the actor with lines to memorize. You'll use a script. You'll think before you speak.

It's sometimes easier to trigger thoughts when we use an acronym. I created N.A.N.A. M.A.E. to help us. She is a gentle older lady in a rocking chair on her front porch and she is asking caring questions.

Take a deep breath, relax, and smile when you answer the phone and think of your ole NANA MAE.

N.A.N.A. M.A.E.

• **N** ame
• **A** ddress
• **N** umbers
• **A** gent and agency
  with another agent
• **M** otivation for calling
• **A** ppointment
• **E** mail address

Here are a few sample dialogues that can help.

RESPONDING TO AN AD CALL

The following is a sample of an actual phone conversation, although the names and addresses have been changed.

Agent: Welcome to ABC Realty. How may I help you?

Caller: I'm calling about an ad I saw in a magazine that says spectacular country home.

Agent: And, what was it about that home that you liked?

Caller: I like the size of the home and that it's on an acre of land. Please just give me an address so I can do a drive-by.

Agent: Oh by the way, I am (FULL NAME), and you are?

Caller: I'm Susan Smith.

Agent: Susan, are you working with a REALTOR® right now?

Caller: No, I'm not. I'm just starting out.

Agent: Well, Susan, you've called on a really nice home that has four bedrooms. Do you need four bedrooms?

Caller: Yes, I do. We have three children and we are looking to relocate closer to the city.

Agent: So, Susan, where do you live now?

Caller: 10 East Main Street, Hometown, CT.

Agent: Do you own that home or are you renting?

Caller: We own our home.

Agent: Would you need to sell that home in order to buy another home?

Caller: Yes, we would.

Agent: I can always give you a complimentary opinion of value on that home for information's sake. By the way, in case we get disconnected, may I please have your phone number?

Caller: Sure, it's (203)555-1212. Could you please just tell me where this home is located so I can do a drive-by? I really don't want to bother you.

Agent: You know you can't judge a book by its cover. I would be happy to show you the inside of that home. It's a really neat property with a lot to offer. I'm available at 3 pm to show you that home, unless later would be better for you?

Caller: I can meet you at 3.

Agent: Why don't you come into my office about 2:45 pm so I can talk to you about that home, and possibly some others that may be of interest to you.

My office is located at 888 Money Street, Friendly, CT. I'll look forward to meeting you this afternoon. I'll see you soon.

Another dialogue example is:

CALLING IN ON A SIGN

The following is a snippet of an actual phone conversation, although the names and addresses have been changed.

Agent: Welcome to ABC Realty. How may I help you?

Caller: I've just driven by one of your "For Sale" signs on Tulip Street and I wonder if you can tell me how much the house is?

Agent: And what was it about that home that you liked?

Caller: It looks like a nice house from the outside and I like the neighborhood. Please just tell me how much it is.

Agent: Oh by the way, my name is (FULL NAME), and you are?

Caller: My name is Billy Buyer.

Agent: Billy, are you working with a REALTOR® right now?

Caller: No, I'm not. I'm just starting out.

Agent: Are you just driving through the neighborhood, or do you live nearby?

Caller: Actually, I live across town on Hoyt St.

Agent: I know Hoyt St. We've done a lot of business over there. What number are you at?

Caller: Number 11.

Agent: That's a nice area. Do you own that home or are you renting?

Caller: I'm renting right now.

Agent: Are you currently in a lease?

Caller: Yes, my lease is up next month. Could you please just tell me the price of that house?

Agent: Yes, I'll get you that information. But in case we get cut off, may I have your phone number?

Caller: Yes, my number is (203) 555-1234. I'm on my cell phone and I might lose you soon.

Agent: That home is listed for $450,000. Is that the price you had in mind?

Caller: Yes, that's around what I thought it might cost.

Agent: I'd be happy to show you that home if you're interested in seeing the inside.

Caller: I don't want to bother you.

Agent: It's no bother. You can't judge a book by its cover. So why don't I take you inside, then you can see all the special features it offers. You have nothing to lose and everything to gain. I am available to meet with you this afternoon, or is tomorrow better?

Caller: I can come in today.

Agent: Great, why don't you meet me at my office at 888 Main Street, My Town, USA. I will look forward to meeting you then.

This will take practice, so that the questions will fall off your tongue easily. When you are looking up information on the property (if you are not already familiar with it,) this is a great time to get to know the caller. By being casual, concerned, and questioning, they will give you a lot of information without ever getting information from you.

If you have trouble with this, just think of the last time you called your dentist when you had a toothache. Did you order him or her to drop everything to meet you now? Would you even think of threatening the dentist with, "If you don't meet me right now, I will go somewhere else?" The office will schedule an appointment for you to see the dentist and you'll hope it is for that day!

Remember, safety first. NEVER, NEVER, NEVER…meet an unknown person for the first time at a listing. This is dangerous and unprofessional. I can tell you dozens of horror stories about agents who met strangers and were harmed. Don't do it! This is for your safety. Any person that is unwilling to schedule an appointment and is difficult would likely be difficult to work with as well.

As I wrote earlier, you will follow much the same technique when responding to emails. Email inquiries should be regarded as internet prospects. The same phone dialogue can apply to emails. You must first get information from them, before giving out information. Again, follow the phone dialogue and simply type it into the reply email… "And what was it about that home that you liked?"

Do not give away your information until you get their information. Wait for a response. Some people will not respond back. There will be others who are serious buyers who will give you a lot of valuable information for you to help them with their home search. Those who answer you are the hot prospects. This is your opportunity to then try to convert the email into an appointment.

Important Dialogue Highlights

- Always answer a question with a question.
- Always start your phone and email conversations by responding to their question with: "And what was it about that home that you liked?"
- To get their name, casually say "Oh, by the way, my name is (Full Name), and you are?"
- Use other key leading questions to get them talking and feeling comfortable with you.
- Close your conversation by scheduling an appointment.

By using these dialogues you will easily be able to obtain the necessary information to proceed with assisting these people in their home search.

The Art of
Negotiations

"The real art of conversation is not only to say the
right thing in the right place, but to leave unsaid
the wrong thing at the tempting moment."

- Dorothy Nevill, *Under Five Reigns*

The dictionary defines negotiation as "to confer with another so as to arrive at the settlement of some matter." Compromise is another good word for this process.

 Everyone loves to be a winner. When it comes to negotiating "deals" we want to win all ways. By perfecting the art of negotiation, your business will be sure to explode.

How often have you heard the phrase: "It's not if you win or lose, it's how you play the game?" I want you to play the real estate "game" so that you are the winner.

Negotiating is the process by which two or more parties with different needs and goals work to find a mutually acceptable solution to an issue. Because negotiating is an interpersonal process, each negotiating situation is different, and influenced by each party's skills, attitudes and styles. We often look at negotiating as unpleasant because it implies conflict, but negotiating need not be characterized by bad feelings, or angry behavior. Understanding more about the negotiation process allows us to manage our negotiations with confidence, and increases the chance that the outcome will be positive for both parties.

Through knowledge and skill, you will change an imperfect you into:

I – AM – PERFECT

I want you to perfect the art of negotiations.
In negotiations one should always talk **WE.**
The word **WE** suggests two parties working together.
The word **WE** hopes for a compromise that will work for all parties.
When we talk **WE,** all parties feel as one.

DEALS DON'T DIE –

AGENTS KILL THEM!
- Ellen Boyle

A strong negotiator is a winner, and a winner is a TOP PRODUCER! This is one of the most important skills we utilize as professionals.

The key here is compromise. Negotiating is overcoming objections together. I always say that when you're one step ahead of the objection, you'll never have to worry about overcoming it.

I've categorized several of the top items that we negotiate in our business. Each will have information on the given topic to follow.

Items we negotiate:

- Commissions/fee for service
- Term of listing agreement
- Contract of Sale/Offer to Purchase
- Purchase price
- Terms of purchase – closing date, items included, home inspection, deposits
- Issues with the home inspection

Negotiating Your Fee for Service

The National Fair Trade Law says our fees are not to be fixed, so we have no choice but to negotiate our fee for service.

I've been asked many times how is it that I have no problems getting paid what I believe I am worth. The answer is easy…I ask for it. There are a few 'tricks' to help you get the fee you desire.

What is *your* service level and what are *you* worth?

When it comes to asking for your fee for service, try asking for *more* than you feel you deserve. Balk at taking less, and settle in the middle. When I negotiate my fee for service I throw out three numbers, and inevitably "settle" for the number I want. In other words if I wanted six apples, I would ask for 5, 6, or 7 apples. Then "settle" for six apples.

The best way to get what you are worth is to go back to your value. What are you worth? Are you valuable?

Value is directly connected with perception. How are you perceived? Are you the BESTT? Hopefully by this point, you've answered YES!!

Why do some people shop for clothing at Talbots and others at T.J. Maxx? Both stores sell clothing. People shop at Talbots because of the high level of service and the quality of their products are top-notch. As soon as a shopper opens the doors at Talbots, all of the staff stop what they are doing to greet you. They offer help if it is needed. When you check out, they thank you for coming in and hope you return soon. The atmosphere is professional, comfortable and inviting.

T.J. Maxx is known for discounts. You don't expect that higher level of service, and you'll settle for less.

There's no reason to discount if you are providing quality service and offer superior skills. Discount brokers have been around for years. When I began in the business, other agents discounted. I never discounted. I knew my value and furthermore, I believed my fellow associate deserved a fair amount for being the cooperating agent in the transaction. When the market is tough, you need your fee even more.

The market time is longer, the amount of money spent on advertising venues is higher, and the time between sales is longer. Now, more than ever, you need your full fee. You will work hard! If you question that, go back to your job description and think about what you do from the time someone first calls you to the closing table. There are many ups and downs, just like a roller coaster ride. And there are no guarantees that you will make a dime until you collect the check at the closing table.

Try using any of these dialogues to overcome the discounters and secure whatever fee you feel you are worth.

- "Some discount brokers pay their employees hourly and NOT on commission! They are paid a standard fee for each transaction. Since their fee is not commission-based, they have no incentive to net you the highest and best price, and you are looking for the highest and best price aren't you?"

- "I know that there are discount brokers who are offering lower commissions. Remember the old cliché, "You get what you pay for." Just think, if they're so willing to give away their money right now, what do you think will happen during the negotiation process when it comes to giving away YOUR money?"

- "By law, all service fees are negotiable. My fee for service is _____ %." (Input your fee.)

- "My fee for service is 3%. What would you like to offer as a co-broke to the selling agent?" (You must explain what a co-broke is and why it is important for each listing to co-broke a full fee of 3%.)

- "With regards to the selling agent's compensation, suppose there are three properties that are all similar. One of these offered a higher compensation to the selling agent. Which property do you think that selling agent would promote?"

- "Let's put aside my fee for service and price opinions. Don't you agree that I have the strongest marketing strategy, and that I would be the BEST REALTOR® to serve you with your real estate needs?"

- If the answer to your question is NO, then ask them WHY?

Use any of these dialogues with the courage of your convictions, and you'll have no problems getting paid what you are worth!

•••

Negotiating Terms of Listing Contract

Regardless of market conditions, general statistics say we need about 6 months to get a property sold. When markets go through downward adjustments, and we have experienced them, I suggest you do what I do and go for a one-year contract.

You'll need as much time as possible for full exposure and extensive marketing. You'll need extra time for the necessary price changes associated with an adjusting market. In every market the sellers always want to try a higher price than you recommend. This will give you an opportunity if there is no activity to get the price to where the market is. Remember that most homes sell within 3% - 5% of the asking price in all markets.

•••

Negotiating the Purchase

There are three simple rules you need to follow when you are working with the buyer.

Rule # 1 – Present in Person

Don't put your business in someone else's hands. The most effective form of selling is FACE to FACE. Get back to the basics. Before fax machines, emails, and text messages, agents actually hand-delivered offers. Imagine that!

To present the offer in person you must first contact the listing agent and say, "I have an excellent offer and **my buyer has instructed me to present the offer in person.**" If you have any concerns about using this dialogue, then ASK your buyer if they would prefer you to email, text, or fax the offer or to present the offer in person.

Ideally, you want to meet with the seller and their agent at the seller's home or in an office to present your buyers and SELL their offer. Regardless of the opening bid, you're the messenger. Remember, everything goes through the listing agent whether in writing, verbally, or in person. This is covered in the REALTORS® Code of Ethics!

Rule # 2 – Build a Strong Presentation Package

The "Buyer Presentation Package" is to include:

- Signed Offer to Purchase.
- Disclosures, where applicable.
- Copy of deposit check, where applicable.

- Bank pre-approval letter with address only. (Do not disclose approval amount, especially if you are offering less than the amount you are approved for. Most bankers will be willing to modify the letter with the address of the property you are bidding on.)

- A handwritten biography of the buyers written by you, the buyer's agent, to humanize them.

- Additionally, have the buyers write a note to express their desire to own this home.

Seal the "Buyer Presentation Package" in an envelope to be delivered to the sellers and their listing agent.

Rule # 3 – Never Email, Text, or Fax Without a Follow-up

These days you will have many agents tell you, "We only email or text." Some agents still do fax. If you have to email or text your offer to another agent, immediately follow up with another email or phone call to confirm that they received it.

When you start taking control of your business and hand-delivering your offers or better yet, presenting in person, you will find it easier to get your offers accepted.

When you meet, it is important to note, you will not open your "Buyer Presentation Package" until you have fully sold your buyers and their offer. The most effective way to get your offer to acceptance is to present the offer from the bottom up. Most Offer to Purchase forms or Offer Contracts are very similar; purchaser name, purchase property and price are on the top, then there is mortgage information, then inclusions/exclusions, closing date, etc. When you start from the bottom, you can get them nodding their heads in a "yes."

So, start by saying, "They'd like to close in 60 days. Is this okay with you?" Hopefully, they nod their heads. You'll continue, "They'd like to have the refrigerator, stove, etc., (all things included on the listing.) Is this okay?" — Heads nodding…

If there are things they do not agree to, ask them, "If we can fix that, would you move forward?" Hopefully, again, the answers are all "yes," and they keep their heads nodding.

You must save the price for last. When you finally reach the offer price, speak the FULL PRICE AMOUNT. So, if your offer is for $450,000, do not say, "Their offer is four fifty." Instead, state the full amount: "Their offer is Four HUNDRED and FIFTY *THOUSAND* Dollars." Then zip your lips, because often the next person that talks… loses.

When you present your offer in this way you have given the homeowner an opportunity to get to know your client, their full offer, and the amount. They can then think it over. Otherwise, they would focus only on the price and nothing else. Once you have successfully presented the offer in person, leave the listing agent and the sellers alone, so they can discuss the offer. Stress your buyer's anxiousness for a speedy reply. Let the sellers know your buyers are waiting by the phone for that reply and possible continued negotiation (only if your buyer has indicated that they are willing to negotiate, or that this is an opening bid.)

You can explain to the seller that you are hoping for one of three things. One, they can accept your offer outright which would be great. Two, they could say "no" outright, and we'll hope that doesn't happen. Or three, they will give a counteroffer (again, if your buyers are open to negotiations.) And this is what we are hoping for.

I will be honest with you, you may encounter resistance from the listing agent to present the offer in person or be unable to present to out-of-town sellers. When this happens, stress your buyer's desire to have the package presented in person. Be persistent. If all else fails, hand-deliver your Buyer Offer Package to the listing agent. Sell the offer to the listing agent and ask to be present while he/she phones the seller.

When you're the listing agent or selling agent remember the unwritten rule that the first offer is generally the best offer. This does not mean it needs to be accepted outright, but it is generally the best offer to work with. As the listing agent, you never know if another offer will present itself. You do not know what tomorrow will bring.

The best proof of this I have is a day we all remember. It was a beautiful Tuesday, with a blue sky and not a cloud in it. I turned on the radio on my way to a class when I heard the news that a commercial plane had crashed into one of the Twin Towers in New York. My first thought was, "How could someone miss such a large structure?" Then, as the news developed throughout the day, the lives of everyone in the world changed. I certainly hope we will never experience another day in history like that day. I often remind clients of the attack when they are hesitant to make a decision. I ask them, "What are you waiting for?"

Using examples like this can help remind people that things can change in a New York minute. Interest rates can rise or drop on any given day. The stock market can crash or have its biggest gain in history. The fact is, we never know what is going to happen, so keeping in the present is what matters.

When you are the listing agent, you should always set the stage to prepare your client for the offer, especially when you have an idea that the offer may be less than the asking price.

I want to remind you again that it is very important to choose your words wisely when presenting offers, speaking with the other agent, and presenting to your own client. Below are some of the top things I have heard agents say when they've called me with an offer that I do NOT recommend that you use if you want your offer accepted.

WHAT NOT TO SAY:

- I've got a terrible offer.
- These buyers are coming in very low.
- These buyers just want to test the waters.
- I've been with these buyers for years and they low-ball everything.
- This is NOT their first choice.

I imagine you're thinking, who would say that? I've actually heard several of them in ONE conversation! Keep in mind that what we do is all about helping other people. Remember that by helping others we help ourselves. Our job is to help someone else get the home of their dreams. This is not our money or our offer, it is our client's. Although it is stepping out of the box in many situations, it works. It doesn't work if we don't work it.

BELOW ARE SOME WINNING STATEMENTS THAT DO WORK – GIVE THEM A TRY:

- I've got great buyers with a great offer.

- This is their opening bid. / This is their initial offer. (Only use if the buyer is looking for further negotiations.)

- My buyers LOVE your home!

- They would love to make this their home.

- They wouldn't change a thing.

●●●

Negotiating Price with the Seller

PRICE is usually the most important aspect of the transaction. We are all interested in obtaining the highest and best price for our sellers and they are interested in netting the most money in their pockets.

One of the biggest challenges you may deal with is the other agent defending 'their' price. The listing agent is defending the asking price. The buyer's agent is defending the buyer's offer. Our work is to get all parties to a meeting of the minds. Our responsibility is to do our best to make these offers work for all parties regardless of our position.

A good negotiator steps out of the equation. They are open-minded and don't take anything personally. This is sometimes easier said than done.

The listing agents must keep in mind that the **asking price** is just that - an ASKING PRICE. It is not the sale price. It is a fake number that won't become real until someone steps up to the plate with money, and then negotiates a price acceptable to both parties. And, like it or not, the buyer establishes the price in the marketplace, not the seller.

Here is some great negotiating dialogue. When negotiating as a seller's agent and the initial offer comes in low, use the following dialogue:

"Mr. and Mrs. Seller, there is an unwritten rule in real estate that the first offer is <u>generally</u> the best offer, and the one you may want to work with. Please listen to my words, as they are "work with." This does <u>not</u> mean you have to accept it without negotiations."

Since many initial offers come in less than the asking price, you need to be ready with more dialogue. Repeat the dialogue to the seller from above:

"Mr. and Mrs. Seller, I know this offer is less than you are asking (pause), and I am hoping for one of three possible responses from you right now:

Number one, you will accept this offer as is, but since the offer is much less than the asking price, I am not expecting a "yes" here.

Number two, you might outright reject this offer and hit me for bringing it to you (chuckle.) (This is a great way to break the ice with the seller and hopefully get you on to number three.)

Or number three, you will give a counteroffer in hopes of getting these buyers up to where you would like them. And frankly, this is what I am hoping for."

Now, be patient and wait for their response. The art of negotiations is addressing every situation with a positive attitude and approach. Again, your mission is to accomplish a win for both parties.

There were too many times in my career when I felt I was on a battleground during negotiations. Do you know what I mean? One party or the other was up in arms and ready for a fight. It's true that everyone wants to be a winner. This is not the time to put on the boxing gloves. Rather, this is the time to use reason. When you keep calm and take charge, everyone wins.

Set the stage for presenting the offer through strategic planning. When you are trying to reason with a seller, be sure to do your homework. Research the date the sellers purchased the house and the price they paid. Try to find out what improvements they made over the years, then go to work. Look up comparable properties that have sold within the last 3-6 months. For example, let's say the property is listed at $500,000. An offer is presented for $450,000. The first thing the seller will say to you is, "I can't afford to LOSE $50,000 by accepting this offer." Your research shows that the seller paid $200,000 for this house 8 years ago, and they put about $25,000 into improvements over the years. So, now what you need to do is put this in black and white and show them the math. Any price over $225,000 will have them making a large gain over their initial investment.

The next question I'm sure you're wondering is what do you do when you encounter sellers who are losing money on their home because they bought in the height of the market, overpaid, or cashed out of their investment early. The most important first step is to ensure that they have monies to cover all of the fees associated with the home sale, including your commission. The next step is to find their motivation for selling, i.e. moving due to extenuating circumstances like a job change, larger family and, of course, short sale and foreclosure. Again, be sure that they can provide proof of funds to cover the costs associated with the sale if it's a short sale or foreclosure.

Spend extra time thoroughly explaining to your seller how market trends affect financial gains or losses. I know this sounds basic, however, many homeowners don't understand the real estate wave. Over the last hundred plus years, real estate has gone up and down. Real estate is a long-term investment, and most people who cash out early stand to lose some money. Those who keep their investment for five to seven years will most likely experience the rising tide and make money over their initial investment.

If their situation appears that their mortgage will convert into a short sale, or even go as far as to be a foreclosure, have them consult with an attorney before listing the property.

Negotiating the Closing Date

The closing date can occasionally be a bone of contention between buyer and seller. Sellers will sometimes want to extend the closing date beyond what the buyer proposed, or vice versa. If this is the case, the negotiator should remind all parties that the quicker the closing, the quicker the sellers have the money in their pocket, the house sold, and the buyers will own their new home.

Here are some possible dialogues to overcome these objections:

- **"The buyer is looking for a 60-day closing. I understand you would like more time to get yourself moved. The truth is that the sooner you close, and have the money in your hands, the better off you are. You never know what may happen in life to change things."**

- **"Maybe we could close on their schedule and propose a rent-back for a bit of time until you get yourself moved out completely."**

- **"Let me remind you that any changes in the contract could cancel the transaction all together. And you do want to sell your house, don't you?"**

Sometimes a buyer can't close sooner because their present home is not under contract. If they are worried about losing the home of their dreams, they may consider making an offer using a Hubbard Clause or obtaining a bridge loan. In either case, I recommend consulting an attorney.

There are many different scenarios, each with a different twist. The important thing is that you are prepared as a negotiator to have a meeting of the minds to keep your transaction going forward.

Negotiating Items Included in the Listing

When negotiating the items to be included in the sale of the property such as light fixtures, appliances, swing sets, etc., it is important as a selling agent and a buying agent to go over every item in detail.

When it comes to appliances, I recommend putting the make and model of the item in writing. It has happened that prior to closing, sellers have switched certain appliances with different and/or older models. Unless there is something in writing, you will not have a leg to stand on if the switch has happened.

Starting with the listing agent, I think it is important for agents to counsel their sellers to remove items from the house that are not staying prior to listing, even if they are planning to swap them out for something similar.

Often when the buyer sees that "Does Not Stay" sign, it triggers something in their head that says, "I MUST HAVE IT."

This situation can be easily avoided by telling the sellers to replace the item with something of equal value BEFORE listing the home.

I had a situation where the sellers did not want to remove a fixture because they were sure it would add some value to the house. However, they did not intend to leave the fixture once the house sold. Turns out, the fixture had intrinsic value but very little monetary value. I tried to encourage them to replace it with a basic fixture prior to listing. They did not listen to me and insisted I tape a "This does not stay." sign to the fixture. When the prospective buyer went through and saw the sign, they were focused on something they couldn't have. When they made the offer on the property, it became such an issue that it almost cost the sale of the house. If the fixture had just been replaced prior to listing, it would never have been an issue.

When you're working on behalf of a buyer, be sure you highlight the items that are, and are not, included. This is especially important when you write up your offer. Don't make the mistake of saying "all appliances." Name each item that is to be included in the purchase or you may be buying a refrigerator at the closing table.

A good rule of thumb for buyers and sellers is that items that are 'nailed down' stay. This includes outlet covers, light fixtures, shower heads, etc. Again, to avoid conflict early, have your seller remove or replace items that are not going to be sold with the home.

•••

Negotiating Issues from the Home Inspection

You should always encourage your buyer to hire a professional Home Inspector to check out the house thoroughly. Many states require the Home Inspector to be licensed. This is an important part of the home buying process. Your buyers will be spending lots of money on their new home and the inspection will help them make a sound business decision.

Whether it's brand new construction or resale, there are often items the home inspector will find that might need to be addressed.

Set the stage with the buyer prior to the home inspection using the following dialogue:

- **"Mr. and Mrs. Buyer, it's important that you understand the home inspection is for <u>your</u> information... and <u>not</u> to be used as a bargaining chip to renegotiate the purchase price."**

You can be sure that *every home, new or old,* has something that will show up as an issue during the inspection. These do not ever have to be "deal breakers." Rather, they are items of negotiation. Now is the time for composure and reasonable compromise from all parties.

The big-ticket items such as roof, heating system, air conditioning, well, septic, foundation, mold, or radon will need to be addressed.

There are several ways to negotiate the major issues that are discovered as a result of the inspection. The seller may be willing to repair the problem(s) totally. This often happens in a "buyer's market" when the seller may want to do whatever it takes to keep the sale. If the seller refuses to make repairs, then suggest splitting the cost with the buyer.

When the buyer does not want to pay any of the costs, ask how they would feel if they lost this home? If they truly found their dream home, they need to be encouraged to be flexible. Splitting the cost means they get something NEW. The fact that they will be living in the house for some time means they have that NEW roof or whatever to enjoy. Splitting the cost works well on items that are not major problems right now, but do need to be repaired.

Whatever happens, do not offer to pay any amount for repairs from your fee. If either party asks for you to "kick something in," simply say:

"I will work hard to negotiate on your behalf and hope WE can make this work, but it is against my policy to kick in money."

Every issue can be worked out. The important thing is that you must persist with the negotiations until you come to an agreement. Don't think of trying an easy out by suggesting the attorneys handle the negotiations. When an agent complains their deal was killed because of the inspection and that they called the attorney for help, I have no sympathy. This is YOUR BUSINESS.

The message here is simply to stay the course and:

PERSIST, PERSIST, PERSIST

•••

Now that you have walked through all of the doors and have the knowledge, you must start to put it to work. Remember to act like a sponge: squeeze out what does not work for you, and keep the rest. Try it all. This business is a challenge, but it has great rewards. One of my favorite quotes from Norman Vincent Peale sums up what I'm trying to say,

"Think enthusiastically about everything; but especially about your job. If you do, you'll put a touch of glory in your life. If you love your job with enthusiasm, you'll shake it to pieces. You'll love it into greatness."

Love Your Work

Love Your Life

In the United States we say, "Do what you love."

In China they say, "Love what you do."

I say, "When you love what you do, you'll never have to work another day in your life."

When I started my career in real estate, a disgruntled associate overheard me say that I was looking forward to the flexibility real estate would offer. That agent chuckled aloud and advised me to be prepared to work "only the days that end in 'Y'." Another associate began chanting the numbers 7-24-365. He said I could count on working 7 days a week, 24 hours a day, 365 days a year, and that would be my flexibility.

Both of those associates had been in the business for several years. They went on to say customers and clients would expect this 7-24-365 level of service. I believed their advice to the extent that I began telling prospects I would be available for them 7-24-365.

Then one day while I was sitting in church, I realized I had a life, and it wasn't all about business. The truth was that I was not always available, and I didn't want to start my business relationship off with a lie.

Today, I tell my clients that I am NOT available 7-24-365, however my VOICEMAIL and EMAIL work around the clock. Tell the truth about your availability. The truth will set you free. The truth will be respected! You will love yourself and your job more, too.

I'll leave you with this final story, a true story from my life. Several years ago when I met with my accountant, Lenny, to prepare my income tax forms, he looked in amazement after seeing my W-2 form showing my income for the past year which was well into a six-digit figure.

He asked if I was working all the time and if I had scheduled any time off for enjoyment. He asked me if I could afford to work less and still be financially comfortable.

After some consideration, I realized I had been working a great deal and had not scheduled much time off. At that point I owned several homes and rental properties, and had a large bank account. I realized I did not need to work so hard and I decided to take more time off. I joined the "vacation of the month club." I was happy, and the kids were happy, too.

The next year I met Lenny again to prepare my IRS taxes. He took one look at my W-2 form and seemed upset with what he saw. My income had increased by 30% over the previous year! He thought that I had not taken the prescribed vacation time. In fact, I had taken more time off than in years past, and I was making more money!

You see, when you enjoy your life, the money will flow. I had visualized financial freedom, and I had it. When I enjoyed my life more, the financial success followed me.

The gift of life is just that. It is a gift for us to enjoy. I don't believe any one of us was born to be miserable. We are here to enjoy. Life is not a dress rehearsal.

Don't be so busy making a living that you haven't got time for a life.

Smell the roses.

Live each day as if it were your last day on Earth.

I love the cartoon quip that says:

> **"Yesterday has passed. Tomorrow is yet to come.**
> **Today is our gift. That is why it is called the PRESENT."**

If you experience a down day, please return to DOOR #1. Repeat your affirmations over and over again. Revisit your purpose for being. Be thankful for all your blessings.

ELLEN'S
MISSION STATEMENT:

To educate, enlighten and elevate you to the highest level of your profession.

Commencement time...

I talk in my classes about the word commencement and that some people think it means the end. **Commencement** really means to begin.

Today is the beginning of the 'NEW DAY' you have longed for.

You possess the power you need to achieve all that you want. Know that when **you go within... you will never go without.**

Take baby steps on your life's journey. The smallest moves will make the biggest changes.

Think of where you started... and stay focused on where you are going.

The doors are wide open for you to reach your dreams. Open your mind and your eyes.

In the words of the well-known author, T.S. Eliot:

"The end of all your exploring will be when you come to where you started and see it for the first time."

I've given you the tools. Now you must take them off the wall and use them!

Suggested Reading

- **The Diamond Cutter** by Geshe Michael Roach

- **Simple Abundance** by Sarah Ban Breathnach

- **The Power of Intention** by Dr. Wayne Dyer

- **How to Win Friends and Influence People** by Dale Carnegie

- **Raving Fans** by Ken Blanchard and Sheldon Bowles

- **Empowerment Takes More Than A Minute** by Ken Blanchard, John P. Carlos and Alan Randolph

- **Feel the Fear and Do It Anyway** by Susan Jeffers, Ph.D.

- **Your Inner Swing** by Randy Friedman

- **Think and Grow Rich** by Napoleon Hill

- **The Hidden Messages in Water** by Masaru Emoto

- **Who Moved My Cheese?** by Spencer Johnson, M.D.

- **The Seven Habits of Highly Effective People** by Stephen R. Covey

- **Do Less, Achieve More** by Chin-Ning Chu

- **The Tipping Point** by Malcolm Gladwell

- **The Secret** by Rhonda Byrne

- **Excuse Me, Your Life is Waiting** by Lynn Grabhorn

- **The Official Guide to Success** by Tom Hopkins

- **The Greatest Salesman in the World** by Og Mandino

- **The Power of Now** by Eckhart Tolle

- **Beyond Selling** by Dan S. Bagley III and Edward J. Reese

- **Chicken Soup for the Soul** by Jack Canfield and Mark Victor Hansen

- **The One Minute Salesperson** by Spencer Johnson, M.D. and Larry Wilson

- **Sell Your Home Faster with Feng Shui** by Holly Ziegler

- **Seven Figure Selling: Proven Secrets to Success from Top Sales Professionals** by Danielle Kennedy